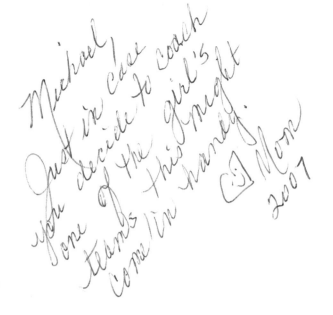

Michael,
Just in case
you decide to coach
one of the girl's
teams this might
come in handy.
♡ Mom
2007

CATCH THEM
BEING GOOD

CATCH THEM BEING GOOD

Everything You Need to Know
to Successfully Coach Girls

Tony DiCicco and
Colleen Hacker, Ph.D.,

with Charles Salzberg

Viking

VIKING
Published by the Penguin Group
Penguin Putnam Inc., 375 Hudson Street, New York, New York 10014, U.S.A.
Penguin Books Ltd, 80 Strand, London WC2R 0RL, England
Penguin Books Australia Ltd, 250 Camberwell Road, Camberwell, Victoria 3124,
Australia
Penguin Books Canada Ltd, 10 Alcorn Avenue, Toronto, Ontario, Canada M4V 3B2
Penguin Books India (P) Ltd, 11 Community Centre, Panchsheel Park, New Delhi—
110 017, India
Penguin Books (N.Z.) Ltd, Cnr Rosedale and Airborne Roads, Albany, Auckland,
New Zealand
Penguin Books (South Africa) (Pty) Ltd, 24 Sturdee Avenue, Rosebank, Johannesburg
2196, South Africa

Penguin Books Ltd, Registered Offices: Harmondsworth, Middlesex, England

First published in 2002 by Viking Penguin, a member of Penguin Putnam Inc.

10   9   8   7   6   5   4   3   2   1

LIBRARY OF CONGRESS CATALOGING IN PUBLICATION DATA
DiCicco, Tony.
    Catch them being good / Tony DiCicco and Colleen Hacker with Charles
Salzberg.
        p.   cm.
    ISBN 0-670-03122-4
    1. Soccer for women—Coaching.   2. Soccer for women—Psychological aspects.
I. Hacker, Colleen.   II. Salzberg, Charles.   III. Title.
GV943.8 .D53 2002
796.334'07'7—dc21   2002025888

This book is printed on acid-free paper. ∞

Printed in the United States of America
Set in Janson Text
Designed by Nancy Resnick

Beyond any other person or group I dedicate this book to my number-one team . . . my family. To my wife, Diane, I'm amazed how much you know about coaching. My four sons, Anthony, Andrew, Alex and Nicholas, are miracles. I get my strength, drive and inspiration from you all.

I love you. How do I say thank you for everything you give me every single day? You are part of every word I write; without you I would have no story to tell.

—*Tony DiCicco*

To my mother, Kathryn M. Hacker, who, throughout my life, "caught me being good" more often than I deserved and continues to do so to this day.

—*Dr. Colleen Hacker*

Acknowledgments

This book has been a wonderful experience for both of us. It allowed us to reflect upon incredible memories, thoughts and emotions associated with our years as coaches with the Women's National Team Program. It also allowed us to remember many of the people who contributed to our success during the 1996 Olympic Games and the 1999 World Cup. Many of these people are mentioned throughout the book but deserve special acknowledgment at this time. Certainly the coaches we worked with had a tremendous impact on the success we enjoyed. Lauren Gregg was there every step of the way. April Heinrichs was the second assistant during the Olympic Gold Medal run and Jay Hoffman was an invaluable assistant during the 1999 campaign, including the Women's World Cup Championship.

Some additional staff whom we worked with, learned from and enjoyed on a daily basis were Dainis Kalnins, Melissa Pilgrim, Brian Fleming, Pam Perkins and, of course, our outstanding press officer and friend, Aaron Heifetz. Our medical team was an amazing asset and included Dr. Doug Brown, Dr. Mark Adams, Dr. Bill Heinz and trainers Sue Hammond and Patty Marchak. It was certainly a privilege to work with and around such an outstanding group of professionals. We truly hope their experience with the team was as rewarding as ours was.

Freqently teams are considered successful only when they win a high percentage of games, although we hope to show in these pages a different set of criteria for judging success. We know that wins happen only when a coach has good players and over the years, our teams were blessed with the best. How could we ever forget the 1995 and 1999 World Cup teams or the 1996 Olympic team? Those players were not only great athletes, but also incredibly unique, gifted and committed individuals. It was nothing less than an honor to work with them all.

Everyone remembers Michelle Akers, Mia Hamm, Kristine Lilly, Julie Foudy, Brandi Chastain and Carla Overbeck. But there is another group, equally as inspiring, that included players like Joy Fawcett, Carin Gabarra, Tisha Venturini, Tiffeny Milbrett, Shannon MacMillan, Briana Scurry, Tiffany Roberts, Tracy Ducar, Saskia Webber, Kate Sobrero, Cindy Parlow, Danielle Fotopoulos, Sara Whalen, Christie Pearce, Mary Harvey and the youngest on the 1999 World Cup Team, Lorrie Fair. This group of athletes and staff share accomplishments and memories with both of us that will only grow in appreciation and amazement as the years go by.

Special acknowledgment is extended to our additional author, Charles Salzberg, the most talented writer among us. Charles always kept us engaged with the material and continually moving forward to our goal. We enjoyed all of our sessions with Charles because he was a sportsman and coach, and we were able to share significant insights. Of course, the real leader for this project was our literary agent, Joelle Delbourgo, who directed us through the entire process with incredible, often inspiring patience. We were blessed to work with the talented professionals from Penguin Putnam, including president Susan Petersen Kennedy, who had the foresight to envision what this book could become long before anyone else did. Sincere appreciation is extended to our exceptional editor, Jane von Mehren, and her assistant, Jessica Kipp, who shared our passion for the project and, with their skill and attention to detail, greatly enhanced the final manuscript.

We hope that our readers learn from and enjoy this book and, perhaps, most important, gain insight into the genuine sense of love and pride we felt in writing it.

Personal Notes

My coaching philosophy is a product of many people who have influenced me throughout my life.

I have to first thank my dad and mom, Tony and Welcome (yes, that is correct) DiCicco. My mom's name was given to her by her parents when they were so happy to have a daughter after having three sons. Both my parents have inspired me, guided me, yet allowed me to choose my own paths. They remain my biggest and most loyal fans.

There have been a select few coaches who were and remain my role models. Coaches like Bob Landers and Lee Bogli who were my soccer coaches at Wethersfield High School in Connecticut. Also Mill Mason, my high school basketball coach, and Charlie Wrenn, my baseball coach. There was also Irv Schmid, the legendary soccer coach of Springfield College. All these men had such a lasting and positive impact on how I teach and coach.

I also had wonderful coaching colleagues during my years with U.S. Soccer. I learned much from Anson Dorrance, Bobby Howe and Glen Myernick. Lauren Gregg was my longtime, very loyal and extremely capable assistant coach. Thanks to all of you. I am inspired by your dedication and insight.

I must mention my staff and friends at SoccerPlus Camp, the camp program that I founded more than twenty years ago and continues to set new standards today, allows me to teach and coach a wonderful collection of motivated student athletes. Thank you, Shawn Kelly, Mich D'Arcy, Januse Michallik and all my directors past and present.

You are all part of this book.

Teaching and coaching are my life and *I love my job!*

—*Tony DiCicco*

Any attempt on my part to acknowledge those who have supported or encouraged my professional life would be an impossible undertaking. Two individuals, specifically in sport psychology, deserve special recognition: Dr. Jean Williams and Dr. Terry Orlick. Jean Williams has served as a mentor, colleague and friend for more than twenty years. Drs. Orlick and Williams have shaped my consultancy work in specific and tangible ways. Readers will note several adapted principles and techniques from numerous books, articles and lectures given by these two outstanding sport psychology specialists. I am grateful and indebted.

I would also like to acknowledge the talented individuals and published resources available through Project Adventure. My formal training in team building occurred primarily through the educational opportunities, including Adventure Education Classes, and written materials provided by Project Adventure. Many of the team-building ideas are adapted from the creative works of Karl Rohnke and Steve Butler in addition to Terry Orlick's *The Cooperative Sport and Games Book*.

In addition, I want to note that many of the team-building activities are modified or refined versions of initiatives and games by Karl Rohnke and Steve Butler in *QuickSilver* (1995) (Kendall/Hunt Publishing Company), *Silver Bullets* (1984), and *Cowtails and Cobras II* (1989)—all by Kendall/Hunter Publishing Company in addition to Terry Orlick's *The Cooperative Sport and Games Book* (1978) published by Pantheon Books, New York.

Finally, I want to thank the remarkable student-athletes at Pacific Lutheran University whom I had the privilege to coach for more than fifteen years. We did something special on the soccer field and we did it *together*.

—*Colleen Hacker*

Contents

Introduction

The Gold Medal game in the 1996 Olympics between the United States and China is, to my mind, the greatest women's soccer game ever played. It was a battle of equals, with everyone playing at the highest possible level. China was more effective than we were in the midfield and we outshone them on defense and in the attack. As a result, it was not unlike a high caliber chess match and, as the game progressed, we were very close to a stalemate. When we got the ball, China couldn't get it. When China got the ball, we couldn't get it. Quite simply, this was an amazing game to watch and even more amazing to be a part of as coach of the Women's Olympic Team.

In the first half we had a wonderful passing combination that started when our goalkeeper, Briana Scurry, distributed the ball up the right flank and it came through Michelle Akers in the midfield. Then we changed the point of the attack to the left flank, to Kristine Lilly, who bent in a terrific cross that Mia Hamm, who was one of the early sequence passers, ran onto and, with the outside of her foot, perfectly placed her volley on goal. Gao Hong, the Chinese goalkeeper, made a great save that hit and ricocheted off the post onto the field. Then Shannon MacMillan opportunistically finished it off, scoring the first goal of the Gold Medal match. It was not only a great passing sequence but also a great finish that included a terrific save by the Chinese goalkeeper.

But China wasn't about to lie down and play dead. Not long afterward, Sun Wen, the scoring phenomenon of the Chinese team, received a long pass over the top that beat our defense. And as Briana Scurry was sprinting out to her, Sun Wen chipped it over her head, but Brandi Chastain, sprinting back, couldn't quite clear it off the goal line. So it was 1–1 going into halftime, and despite the fact that it was a tie, I was still loving the game because everyone was playing so incredibly well.

I had very little to say to the team in the locker room because we were doing so many things well. After the normal tactical adjustments I told the players that they had been a great group to coach over the last year and that now it was up to them. They had forty-five minutes to fulfill their dream of winning the first ever Olympic Gold Medal for women's soccer, and although we'd played well, we needed to play better to defeat this worthy opponent. In fact, I was so excited and so eager for the second half to begin that after only a few minutes I left the locker room and went back onto the field. After a moment or two of standing alone in front of our bench, in front of thousands of fans, I began to feel a little exposed, suddenly realizing that here I was the head coach but my team was still in the locker room.

When the team returned for the second half, I was not disappointed by the quality of play, which had all the drama you would expect from two great teams. Once again we had a great passing sequence with Mia Hamm passing to Joy Fawcett, who was coming out of defense. We must have completed twenty passes in a row, trying to build our attack through the left flank, bringing it back and trying the right flank. China stole the ball—they got it for perhaps one pass—and then we stole it back again, and while they were expanding players out of their defense, we sneaked in on them. Joy Fawcett, with perfect timing and tremendous speed, beat the last defender and slid the ball across the face of the goal to Tiffeny Milbrett, who scored the go-ahead goal, making it 2–1.

After Tiffeny scored the goal, I took her out of the game and, as a defensive move, put in Tiffany Roberts. There were about twenty minutes to go in the match and in these kinds of games the last twenty minutes are hell. The other team is sending everything it has forward and your team's back is up against the wall. But in this instance we took the game over by maintaining possession of the ball so that the Chinese team had to keep chasing it and us. By the last five or ten minutes, in my mind at least, the game was over. In fact, I made a substitution, a gesture of respect, by putting in Carin Gabarra, one of the great stars of women's soccer and a Hall of Famer, to give her the opportunity to play in the Olympic final. She deserved to be in the game, but under normal conditions a coach would not have substituted an offensive player at that point in the match. For me, however, the maneuver showed the high level of confidence I had in our team. I knew there was nothing to stop us.

That Gold Medal contest was the epitome of the game of soccer, and our team played like a perfectly scripted dream. I remember sitting on the bench and marveling at what was happening on the field. Every pass I thought we should be making, we made. Every shot we should have been taking, we took. There was a connection I had with the team and the way they played that was really an enactment of how I thought they should play. We were a team on our competitive edge, playing at an extremely high level of skill tactically, physically and mentally. For ninety minutes we played the game just about as well as it could be played.

How were we able to reach that level of play, and how were we able to maintain excellence over such a long period of time? There are no simple answers, of course. And to understand the significance of our dominating play and win in 1996, we have to look back to 1992, my second year as a member of the coaching staff and the year after our first World Cup win. We played only two games that year, and none of our World Championship team members competed except Mary Harvey and Mia Hamm. In 1993 the team was beaten three times, twice by Germany and once by Norway. And then we lost in the World University games to China, 2–1. So the telltale markings were there—we were no longer the best team in the world, and yet, technically speaking, we were still reigning World Champions.

A pretty good year for us was 1994, when we won a domestic tournament, beating Germany 2–1, China 1–0 and Norway 4–1. But the truth is, in that 4–1 game against Norway, the score could easily have been reversed. For the first forty minutes we were totally dominated by the Norwegians, although they didn't score. Just before halftime I substituted Michelle Akers, and she turned the game around. With Michelle in the game we managed to sneak in a goal and then another one at the start of the second half. In effect, we "stole the game" from them. Despite winning that tournament, I could see there was something lacking in our play. Without domestic leagues, without the players having the luxury of training on a regular basis, we were losing ground to the rest of the world.

When I took over as coach of the women's team in the summer of 1994, I knew we weren't the best team in the world. One of the roadblocks we had always faced was that we would meet as a team for only a week or ten days during a tournament or spend numerous days in training but then play just one match. That changed in February of 1995, when we finally became a residential team and moved our training camp to Florida. Even more important than establishing our own facility, I felt, was the need to strengthen our mental skills. When I was a player, I was a goalkeeper, a position that is 90 percent mental and 10 percent physical. As a result of my experiences playing that position, I've always believed that when you reach a certain level in athletics, the difference between success or failure is determined by mental skill. That's the trump card because by that time players are technically proficient, and they understand the tactics of the game and are physically prepared.

I wanted to hire a sport psychologist to address our mental skills before the World Cup in June. We brought in two or three different people to address the team. Then, in May, about six weeks before the World Cup, we had a trip out west to play Brazil, in Tacoma and in Portland. While we were there we had a chance to have Dr. Colleen Hacker work with the team. I already knew Colleen by her national reputation as an authority on the psychology of peak performance and team building and from working with her at the National Soccer Coaches Association. Colleen also had soccer expertise from having been a coach at Pacific Lutheran University, where her teams won numerous conference, district and regional championships as well as three national women's collegiate soccer titles between 1988 and 1991. I was aware that she taught and trained teams to use psychological skills effectively—to use imagery, set goals, manage stress, build concentration and focus, and control distractions. By implementing creative and appropriate risk-taking situations, she could foster absolute trust among players and nurture their cohesion as a team. Colleen joined us in Oregon and Washington and conducted a team-building and mental skills training session. When I heard her speak, I could see that she had a special connection with the team, a way of dealing with the players that they responded to immediately.

When we got home, I spoke to officials at the United States Soccer Federation: "I'd like to bring a mental skills coach to Sweden with us for the World Championship and I'd like it to be Colleen Hacker." The idea was immediately shot down. I was told it wasn't in the budget and, besides, it was relatively late in the preparation period. But there was still more than a month to go and I thought Colleen could definitely give us an edge.

As it turned out, we lost a very close game in the semifinals. We were not assertive in that game, at least in the first half. We had a couple of young players who were not in the right place mentally. I had tried to get them there, but I wasn't completely successful. When we lost that tournament and came away with the Bronze Medal, I was even more convinced that if we were to regain our status as the best team in the world by the 1996 Olympics, we needed to secure a sport psychologist.

The officials at U.S. Soccer still didn't approve the hiring of Colleen, but fortunately, because the United States Olympic Committee wanted to do whatever it could to give the top American teams an edge, it created a program called Home Team Grants, designed especially for teams that had a chance to medal. So when they came to me and asked what I needed, my answer was simple: "I need a video editing system and I need a sport psychologist," and that meant Colleen Hacker. Eventually they agreed to both requests, and Colleen joined the team about six months before the Olympic Games started.

In one of our first conversations Colleen said to me, "I'm going to offer individual meetings to all the players, but I want it to be completely voluntary." Her hope was that players would want to commit to mental skills and training and not feel as though they had to in order to please her or the coaching staff.

"I know who the last player will be to take you up on an individual meeting," I said. "It's Mia Hamm. She's a very private person, she's shy and I know it isn't something she will jump on. Some of the other players want to talk everything out, but Mia holds a lot of it in. She's got to *really* feel bonded to a person, and she's got to *really* feel a trust before she's going to open up."

About a month later we were at the Olympic Training Center, and Colleen, who had been training with us on a regular basis, had already set up a number of individual player meetings. She was winning over the players wonderfully, but she still hadn't met with Mia. One day I noticed that Mia was talking privately to Colleen on the sidelines. They weren't actually having a meeting, but I could tell this was the groundwork for setting one up. Later that day I approached Colleen and said, "I saw you talking with Mia today and I think that's great!"

What Colleen created was a safe place for the players to speak about me, the team, the training, their performance, the grind of being away from husbands and families and whatever else had the potential for negative impact on their performance. Colleen *became* that safe and trusted place and as a result she became very, very valuable in every aspect of mentally preparing our team to win. I was preparing them physically and technically, teaching them tactics to be used in the game, but Colleen was preparing them psychologically. Without Colleen it was as if we were a chair with only three legs—wobbly and unreliable. But with four legs, and Colleen providing the fourth leg, we were steady and held our own weight. After Colleen implemented the mental skills training program, we went into the Olympics a different team, a more prepared team, a better team. And when we came out we were Gold Medalists and the best team in the world.

The missing piece Colleen added to our team in 1996 was the thing that made us so special. We couldn't have played at that higher level a year earlier because we didn't have the mental edge. And it wasn't just the mental skills: It was the preparation, the confidence, the psychology of long-range commitment and peak performance training—and a willingness to be successful. Colleen was able to find the pulse of our team which allowed her to identify the key in each player that facilitated her understanding that she had more to give than she knew. This process allowed them to release some incredibly powerful, but hidden energies that each one possessed.

In order to help the reader take advantage of Colleen's expertise, at the end of each chapter we've included exercises she used with the Women's National Team to foster a sense of cooperation and to strengthen necessary skills that are important in creating a successful team. Each exercise is keyed to the particular chapter. The lessons we learned throughout our journey can, I believe, be applied not only to the elite players I coached, but also to female players whether six, thirteen or twenty-four.

We've also included a series of Chalk Talks that cover topics ranging from dribbling to heading to passing to shooting and scoring. These Chalk Talks are not designed to provide A to Z answers for coaches, but rather to stimulate and inspire them to come up with their own creative ideas on how to best prepare their team for the season.

The aim of this book is to teach coaches, parents and the players themselves the winning techniques that have worked for us. We hope that by using and understanding these techniques, parents can help their daughters attain their goals. We also want to show the girls that it's all right to compete and that they can do so at the highest levels and succeed.

During the years I've coached women I've learned a lot about myself, and with the help of my players, my family and especially my wife, Diane, and Colleen Hacker, I think I've evolved into a better coach, one who knows that there's more to the game of soccer, to any sport for that matter, than simply x's and o's. It's about competing. It's about winning. But perhaps most of all, it's about having fun and enjoying the journey along the way.

CATCH THEM
BEING GOOD

CHAPTER 1

My Coaching Philosophy

The objective in any team sport is to transform the group from a mere collection of talented individuals into a highly cohesive unit so that the whole is greater than the sum of its parts.

—COLLEEN HACKER

Even before stepping onto the field for tryouts or the first day of the season, you should know, as a coach, how you are going to approach the game. Think of it as a game plan on a larger scale, a blueprint for the kind of coach you want to be. Over the years I've been asked many times what my coaching philosophy is, so I've tried to sum it up here as succinctly as possible, breaking it into ten rather simple principles. Taken together these principles show how I approach teaching and coaching.

1. Know Your Limitations and Use Them as Strengths

Whatever you do, do it to the best of your best ability. This sounds obvious and maybe even a little simplistic, but its very important corollary is that you must understand what your best abilities are and then work with them. In other words, in order to perform at the highest level, you have to know your limitations and at the same time use your strengths.

Being aware of your limitations allows you to enhance your performance by surrounding yourself with the best people, which is what I've always done. Frankly, I've seen a lot of people do the opposite. People who are afraid their abilities will be undermined are threatened by the talents of others. And I have to admit that at times, I've felt that way too. It can be pretty scary to be surrounded by people more talented in some areas than you are, but in the end I've always tried to appreciate my own abilities and those of my coaching colleagues to allow us to do what was best for the team to help us win.

Surround yourself with talented people who understand their role in the larger scheme of things. If you have a tremendous talent with a big ego who goes behind your back or works behind the scenes to try to undermine what you're doing with the team, that person is undermining the team. I've always brought in talent who understood the role they'd be playing. Sometimes I brought in people who had different opinions about the game or what should be done in certain circumstances so I could learn from them and, in turn, they could learn from me.

I've always tried to be the kind of leader who brings in other leaders. At the same time, I have to be sure they're loyal, that they keep the team as their number-one focus so that together we can achieve success. In my experience, whenever I've enjoyed success it wasn't just my success but also that of Colleen Hacker, Jay Hoffman, Lauren Gregg and April Heinrichs, all of whom were an integral part of my coaching staff. And in the end this is why we won: Each of them brought to the table unique talents that complemented my skills.

If you're coaching at a the nonprofessional level or the equivalent of a youth soccer team, you're probably not going to have the luxury of surrounding yourself with experts. In that case, the best thing you can do is learn as much about the game as possible. In terms of tactics, there are a number of books or videotapes that can help prepare you for the season. It's also a good idea to watch as much soccer, both at the professional and amateur level, as you can.

2. Play Hard, Play to Win, Have Fun

You must teach your team to play hard, no matter who the opponents are, because you're setting your own standards, playing toward goals you want the team and each player to achieve. Your players must learn that the best respect they can give opponents is to play to win, to show them their best.

When I look back, one of the things I'm proudest of is not the record of our team—103 wins, 8 losses and 8 ties over a five-year period—but that we had a winning record against every opponent and that no team beat us that shouldn't have beaten us. To me that's unique because at times it's easy to play down to your opponent's level, to leave some of the key ingredients that make you special out of your play.

Playing to win doesn't mean that winning is the end-all, but it's an important component of success. And yet the game is still just that, a game. You need to keep things in perspective and communicate that approach to the players. We're not conducting open-heart surgery or flying a plane with only one engine or performing heroic acts the way firefighters, police officers and our military personnel do every day. But in the heat of the moment of the Big Game, winning is certainly very important. If you're coaching or playing in a Gold Medal game, it will be one of your most important accomplishments. Even then it's still a game, and no one's going to live or die because of it. All too often, coaches and parents take the fun out of the game, and when that happens you might as well have your team play with a weight on one foot, because you're making it that much harder to achieve and enjoy success.

Remember, most of the players you're coaching are not going to go on to the highest level of competition or even to the collegiate level. If you create an environment of fun in which your players appreciate physical activity and learn the game and teamwork and strategy, you will teach them discipline, team chemistry and confidence-building skills that will translate into other areas of their lives.

3. Less Is More

The phrase "less is more" was something we said during the Olympic and 1999 World Cup buildup. Ours was an incredibly fit and mentally focused team, a team trained to peak performance that resulted in winning games. What we learned from many Olympic athletes and some of the Olympic and National team coaches, however, was that at some point they did too much, and as a result they didn't achieve the success they might have otherwise. When asked what they would have done differently, athletes who underachieved often said, "I would probably not have overtrained in the last month."

So when you're at the final stages of preparation for the big tournament or game, back off from the physical training a bit and spend more time fine tuning, making sure everyone is confident. If you've prepared properly, you'll actually get more out of it.

4. The Relay Paradigm

There have been studies that show that exceptional swimmers are actually faster when they swim 100 meters as part of a relay team than when they are in an individual race. It seems that as part of a team an athlete gathers support from the other team members, which makes the individual better. In other words, as a part of the whole, performances are raised, and that's the relay paradigm, as Colleen refers to it. The effective coach nurtures these performance-enhancing team relationships so that the team's performance is better than the sum of its players' talent and coach's leadership.

5. Vulnerable, Humble Leadership

There are many successful leadership models, but some of them are now outdated. For me these would include the methods used by coaches such as Bobby Knight, Mike Ditka or the former Ohio State football coach, Woody Hayes. These are leadership models that in large part traffic in intimidation tactics. Many of their players loved these coaches, obviously, so there was certainly a side of them that was very positive, but they also had the presence of demigods, and that clearly won't work when coaching girls or women. My leadership style is very different: I believe it's important to show players that I'm not perfect, that I make mistakes.

Showing my vulnerability, I believe, allows me to inspire players and doesn't separate them from me. It's important that players know you understand some of the insecurities and challenges they're going through, and you can do this only if they see your own vulnerability. So when you make a mistake, and we all do, ask yourself if you can admit that you made that mistake. Or are you caught in that place where you say, "I am a leader and I can never question myself or put myself in a position where I can be challenged in my leadership"?

To my way of thinking, being an infallible coach is far less effective than admitting your vulnerabilities and leading through your humanity. This is not a new leadership style: John Wooden and Phil Jackson exemplify this model.

6. Validate Their Feelings

Validating a person's feelings is something I learned while working with women. It is a method of interaction that optimizes listening skills. For example, when somebody comes to you and says, "I've had a terrible day. I went to a meeting and found I was an hour late." They don't want to hear you say, "Well, you know, I have a great pocket notebook that works for me, and it's really kept me organized." What they want is for you to say, "You must feel terrible about that. You probably feel like you let people down. I'm sure they're going forgive you though, because they know what type of person you are." This way, you're validating and sharing those feelings or, as Colleen might say, "wearing" those feelings with them.

Let me give you an example of something that happened with Mia Hamm when I took over the team in 1995. We were playing in a tournament in France and, admittedly, I was overcoaching from the sideline. I was trying to tell the team, and specifically a certain player, the runs and tactics from the sidelines that I felt should be made. At one point Mia, who's a lot like me in that we're both fiery people, came over and said, "Tony, just let her play."

I thought Mia was really displaying a lack of respect and I said a couple of not-so-nice things to her, and then when she made a bad play I yelled out to her and kind of dug in the knife a bit. At halftime Mia was visibly upset with me, and I wasn't about to change the way I was feeling either. I was ready to take her out of the game, but when we got back on the field, Carla Overbeck, our captain and a tremendous leader, came up to me and said, "I know you're really upset with her, but let's keep her in the game. This is how we're going to get her back." I thought a moment and then said, "All right, Carla, let's give your idea a try." My agreement with Carla not only empowered her and helped our relationship, but it also avoided a rift between Mia and me that could ultimately affect the whole team.

I always have individual meetings with players on tournament game days. I knew that Mia would probably be dreading coming in to meet with me for our one-on-one time before the next game. And the truth was, I was dreading seeing her. But in the interim I was able to think about how she felt and the effect of my actions. And as hard as I tried not to, I kept coming up with the inescapable conclusion that Mia was right: I was overcoaching. I hated to believe that, but it was true.

So when she came in for our meeting, I said, "You know, Mia, we have to talk about the other day."

"I know. I know," she said.

"Look, I've given it a lot of thought and I think there are a couple of things we have to talk about, but the bottom line is, and I need to tell you this, I think you were right. I did overcoach."

The look on her face was as if I'd said, "Mia, here's a thousand dollars." And that's because what I did was validate what she felt, and what she saw. The next few moments were filled with apologies back and forth: "I overreacted, I shouldn't have said what I said." "Well, you know, I did the same thing."

Mia left and in our game that night she put on quite a show, scoring a hat trick. We destroyed Canada. Afterward the staff wanted to know what I had said to her. I remember the team doctor coming up to me, looking for some gem and asking, "How did you get her to play like that?"

"Well, I sat her down and said, 'You know, Mia, I think you're right.'" He just loved that because he recognized it as coming from a place of strength, showing that I could be vulnerable, that I could validate Mia's feelings, and that I had taken the time to really evaluate the whole situation and be objective about it. I know that for Mia and for me, instead of forcing us apart, the incident actually improved our relationship.

In effect, what I did was to try to put myself in Mia's place, to *validate* her feelings, which then empowered her.

7. The Challenge Coefficient

Whatever you do, you must create challenge, especially if you want growth from your players and your team. And it's got to be a real challenge. Colleen stresses the importance of optimally challenging athletes in all aspects of the game. The demands placed on players must be carefully balanced between their actual skills and abilities. Sometimes I see challenges that are merely tokens, and players see through them and are not impressed by them. The challenge needs to stretch them individually and collectively, but the secret is to make sure your players are successful.

You must make the challenges realistic and applicable, and hard enough that the team is not sure they can complete it. When you help guide them to success, they will recognize their ability and you will have created a situation in which the team and each player can say to herself, "I didn't know if I could do this, but I did it. I feel good about myself."

When you produce a challenge that your players successfully meet, you're building self-esteem and self-confidence, and there's often a direct correlation between self-confidence and performance. The higher the self-confidence, the higher the performance. If your players are not successful, you may be overtraining them in some physical or tactical aspect or, alternatively, perhaps you need to structure more optimally challenging, successful experiences for them in order to boost their confidence and positive expectations.

8. Imprint Versus Perfect

I'm a perfectionist in a lot of ways, but I also understand performance dynamics. For competitive athletes the ideal is always to perfect every aspect of their game, but it doesn't always work the way you want it to. For instance, let's say I tell Shannon MacMillan, "I want you to drive this corner kick across the goal. I want you to put it right here, on Joy Fawcett's head." Now she's 45 or 50 yards away when I say this. Joe Montana would have a lot of trouble throwing a football that far and that accurately, and yet I'm asking Shannon to kick the soccer ball right there.

I could ask her to do it, and do it, and do it again to try to get to that level of perfection, but it's unrealistic. It would be equally un-realistic if you said to Joe Montana, "Throw this pass to this exact spot every single time." It's a 40-yard pass and he's probably good enough to do it a percentage of the time, but he can't do it a hun-dred percent of the time. What you have to understand as a coach, a parent and a player, is that you're not going to get perfection. What you're really looking for, then, is not perfection but under-standing. You want to *imprint* what you're trying to do. Now if Shannon's first kick hits Joy Fawcett in the head, right where I wanted it to be—which, by the way, was the winning goal in the 1999 World Cup quarterfinal against Germany—we're done. That's it. I'd say, "Does everybody understand their roles, their runs and everything? Are we okay with that? Now, let's go to the other side and we'll do it from there." If Shannon takes three or four kicks and misses them by 15 yards, we don't keep going till she makes it. In-stead, I might say, "If you understand where we want you to put the ball, we'll be fine on game day. Does everybody understand their runs? Great, let's move on."

This is the difference between imprinting and perfecting. I see a lot of coaches who always demand perfection. You can approxi-mate perfection, but you can't achieve it in one session and you can't execute at that level all the time. Sure you can practice a skill, a technique or a play fifty times until you do it perfectly, but if you do that, you've lost your team mentally, and for the rest of the day you're going to have to battle to keep their heads focused on training. When you do a particular exercise two or three times— knowing it's not perfect but knowing that it's a layering process— and then repeat it during subsequent practices, it will eventually pay off. This is what imprinting is all about.

9. One Size Doesn't Fit All

Coaching style is dependent upon the people and the circumstances. Every player and every team is different because of criteria like where they are in their physical and mental development and who their opponents are. You can't coach to a stereotypical athlete. The goal is to try to get your team members to be somewhat similar without taking away their individuality, or their special skills. Coaching Brandi Chastain and Michelle Akers simultaneously was a very rewarding but a completely different experience. I had to push Brandi harder to bring out the world-class player she is; whereas with Michelle, because of her health, I had to back off and give her a lot of autonomy with her training regimen. What is constant, however, is that you build your team through the union of each individual's uniqueness.

In other words, you cannot coach successfully to a common denominator. The Philadelphia 76ers can't win if they have five Allen Iversons on the court, no matter how great a player he might be. Similarly, you can't be successful if you coach every player on the team the same way you coach Iverson. You need a Dikembe Mutombo, and you need other kinds of players to fulfill their roles as well. Everybody has a different trigger, everybody has a different skill set and everyone's going to have a different responsibility in the game.

You have to know your team, not just as a group of players but as separate people. That's where the real triggers are—not just in their game personalities, but also in their human personalities.

10. Be Prepared to Take a Penalty

If the World Cup had gone into penalty kicks in 1991, I seriously doubt that we would have been victorious. That's because we had a team stigma that said, "We can't make penalty kicks." From my perspective, this was a cop-out. It resulted from not being prepared mentally to do whatever we needed to win. I remember Kristine Lilly's comment: "I hope we never have to go to penalty kicks. We better always win in regulation." What she was really saying was, "We suck at penalties."

I saw this attitude as a problem and even as early as 1992 we started to talk about it. "Someday we're going to have to win in penalty kicks," I said, "and you know what? You're going to have to prepare yourself physically and mentally to win them."

As we got closer to the big events, I coined this phrase, "Be prepared to take and be prepared to make a penalty kick." In 1995 we didn't have to go to penalty kicks. In 1996 we didn't have to go to penalty kicks, but we still used the saying throughout our Olympic buildup.

I always thought we had a fifty-fifty chance of having to go to penalty kicks sooner or later, but I never thought we'd have to do so in the final of the biggest women's sporting event in history. But we did. Five players stood up on the field of the Rose Bowl on July 10, 1999, before more than ninety-one thousand fans and a billion viewers worldwide. And those same five players walked from the center circle to the penalty spot, took their penalty kicks and scored.

In our case the fear of taking penalty kicks simply represented a lack of confidence that, in turn, became a self-fulfilling prophecy. In order to succeed, your players must be confident. Fear of failure is not and cannot be an option. Once the players *believed* they could make the penalty kick and understood that sooner or later they would *have* to take a penalty kick, they *did* make the penalty kick.

The point here is that we didn't get to 5 for 5 overnight. In fact, preparing for what we accomplished in the World Cup final of 1999 took years, but when the players did finally internalize the knowledge that they could make those penalty kicks when they had to, it created a collective memory for a sporting nation.

I've tried to use these ten principles to guide me through my coaching career and I believe that if you, as coaches and parents, apply them wisely, you'll have a successful winning season.

CHAPTER 2

Girls Sweat Too: The New Model of the Champion

Society often positions women to just fit in. We coach them, however, to stand out, to make a difference, and for women that can be an incredibly empowering experience.

—TONY DiCICCO

When Mia Hamm was asked by the press how she wanted herself and her teammates to be coached, she replied, "Coach us like men, treat us like women."

It may seem as if Mia intended to emphasize that men and women are different, but I don't believe that's the case. Instead, what I think she meant was, "Don't think that we, as women, can't compete at the same level of intensity as men do. And don't think that we, as women, can't train at the highest level of fitness as men do. We can, and we want to. We don't want to be coached differently and we don't *need* to be coached differently. So coach us as you would coach the most elite men's team. And at the same time, treat us like women, which means don't be in our faces, don't be confrontational. Challenge us, but do it in a humanistic way."

Mia was referring to what I think of as the model of the new champion, which in terms of coaching simply means using a more humanistic approach. In using the phrase "Treat us like women," she was alluding to characteristics and traits that we usually associate with women but certainly are not limited to one gender: emotional intelligence, compassion, empathy, the ability to listen and to relate to others. Traditionally, the characteristics most commonly attributed to men have been egocentrism, aggressiveness, intensity, assertiveness and overall macho behavior.

I believe that in order to create the new model of the champion, we, as coaches and as parents, must combine the best qualities of women with the best qualities of men. If we do, we'll come up with an incredible athlete like Julie Foudy, who is aggressive, tough, intense, assertive, fit and competitive and finds a way to win while being relational, empathetic, compassionate and nurturing.

The Old Model

In order to fully understand the new model of the champion, we have to take a look at the old one. These teams tended to be coached by people like Woody Hayes, former football coach at Ohio State, and Bobby Knight, former basketball coach at Indiana and currently the head coach at Texas Tech. Both these coaches espoused a hard-core, get-the-whip-out macho mentality. They were tough on their players, driving them to compete at the highest possible level. They set high standards and insisted that their players reach those standards. For the most part, they did not distinguish one player from another—they treated each of their players the same way, relentlessly driving them to perfection.

In terms of wins and losses, these coaches were successful and their methods got results—at least in the short run. This way of relating to athletes might be fine for some individuals, but it must be balanced with other types of human qualities and different techniques for motivation. Otherwise it becomes a very narrow and limited way to see the world. And any time you limit your vision, you reduce your chances for success. We need to create greater balance in our leadership style and understand that there are a multitude of ways to relate to those who may need more than the iron fist to be motivated. As society has changed so have athletes. No longer do they blindly accept fiats on how to do things. They often ask why. And coaches need to realize that not all people are the same. There are different ways to motivate different kinds of personalities. The whip might work for some, but a less strident, more nurturing approach might work for others. Young girls, for instance, aren't used to this kind of harsh, confrontational treatment, so rather than blossom they will probably shrink into a shell or simply quit the team. And it isn't only girls, many boys also react the same way.

There was a time when we, as coaches, would not allow our players to ask why we wanted them to do something. The answer was always, "Just do it because I told you to." At times, that may still be the best answer, but if we're trying to develop young women who can think on their feet, and certainly this is true in the game of soccer, you have to foster your players' ability to make decisions on the spur of the moment. So, as a coach, you must let your players ask why you're having them do something a certain way. If we're asking players to make decisions, they'd better know *why* we're asking them to make those decisions.

I always appreciated it when my team felt comfortable enough to come and speak to me, to ask me for advice or even to tell me about a problem they were having. To me, the epitome of coaching is having the kind of rapport in which your players are comfortable enough to come in and say to you, "I'm struggling out there and I just don't know how to pull myself out of it." Or even when they say, "Coach, can I give you some feedback?" and then tell me, "You're yelling at us a lot. You're being very critical. It's not as much fun right now." I think when that happened, and it did happen, that's when I knew that my coaching had matured to this new model. And at times, the personal interchanges with my players were better than wins and losses.

But it wasn't always this way. In the past, I had tried to lead with my own intensity instead of inspiring my players with my humanity. At times I had been overly critical and although I found that being critical sometimes achieved results, being positive and finding the coaching moments was more effective.

This new model of champions that we're seeing emerge is, I think, the direct result of Title IX of the Education Amendments of 1972, which gave women the same right to federal funding, coaching, facilities and equipment for sports previously earmarked only for men. Essentially, this sent the message, which has grown slowly, that it's okay for women to compete, sweat and be tough, physical and assertive. As we start coaching to the full range of qualities in each person, we end up with a more successful, elite athlete who can deal with adversity, live with different roles within the team and contribute to tactics.

In the end, striking a balance by using the best characteristics of men and of women makes for a better way to lead and a better way to influence and foster a higher level of performance. It's not really a question of abandoning the old model, it's simply a matter of infusing and applying the strength from both models to complement and support each other.

Exchanging Your Old Model for the New One

If you're used to coaching a particular way, it's not easy to shift gears. There are certain steps you can take, however, that will put you on the right track toward encouraging the new model of champion by incorporating your own leadership style.

Creating Competition

Historically, young girls don't have the support that boys do when it comes to competitive team sports. I think that's changing quickly, but until it does you must be careful about how you introduce the game. For generations, boys have been taught to be competitive and are assured that being so doesn't necessarily damage the relationships they're going to have with their opponents or even their own team members. We must permit, and also encourage girls and young women to be competitive as well. Parents and coaches have to convince girls and young women that just because they're competing on the field doesn't mean that this competition is going to hurt their friendships and relationships off the field.

One of the methods a coach can use to instill competition among girls is called keeping score, which is a concept that was introduced to me by the legendary University of North Carolina coach, Anson Dorrance. At the end of each practice or team scrimmage, the coach tells the team who the top winners are for that day. Gradually, players come to learn that if their names aren't on the list, they're going to have to compete a little harder the next time. It's the same approach you might use with the super student who comes home from third grade after turning in all her homework assignments on time and thinks that was all she was supposed to do. Her role isn't to get the homework done and coast. The idea is to inspire her to give every effort possible, to work hard to try to reach the highest standard possible. If a child's name isn't on that list of achievement, moms and dads say, "Gee, I'd really like it if your name were on that list. What can we do to help you reach a higher standard and be more successful?" What we're doing here, whether we know it or not, is asking our children to compete, even if it's competing against the best standard possible for that individual in that particular situation.

Competition is a great way to have fun, to learn about yourself, to grow in self-esteem. But we can also turn competition into a negative thing, particularly if we overemphasize it. The key is to include opportunities for players to compete against their previous best performance, against some objective standard, as well as against others. I believe that by using competition I can make practices a lot more fun and engaging than I can without it. And as a coach, I think one of the best things we can do to raise all of our players' self-esteem is to occasionally create competitions in which those players who usually don't make the top of the Keeping Score list can do so. For instance, instead of having players compete against each other, have them compete against themselves. Those who better their previous performance, make the list.

Asking Advice

Ask advice of your captains and other leaders. Don't be afraid to say, "You know, I'm thinking of doing this tomorrow, and it's going to be a pretty tough training day. What do you think?" By using this method you will appropriately empower your team, and I guarantee their answer will be, "We can handle it." Or their response might be, "Can we do that the next day so we can let our legs recover?" When that "next" day comes up, they're going to really go after it. Because it was their idea, it becomes a commitment they've made to you and they won't let you down.

By empowering your players, you get them to buy into your coaching plan. By giving your players what Michael Useem calls leadership moments, no matter how small, you develop leadership.

Learning to Listen

I am a teacher by trade and the one thing I learned early on—and believe me, it wasn't easy—was how to listen. More specifically, I learned that when someone comes to us with a problem, we should immediately think about possible solutions. When a player seeks your help with a problem, don't make judgments and don't make quick decisions or offer immediate suggestions. Instead, just listen. This can make all the difference in the world in your overall relationship with your player, and it will facilitate your ability to lead.

Listening is important because it increases your ability to relate to your players. It also gives you time to figure out how a player is feeling and to consider plausible, alternative explanations for behavior. If a player is acting out or not training at the level you expect, it might not be that she's simply trying to avoid training. There could be other explanations. Good leadership and good coaching do not mean scanning the surface and saying, "Lack of training = punishment." You have to find the underlying reason for the problem, and you can only do that by actually listening to your players.

Being Flexible

There's no reason why coaching has to be rigid. If you simply say, "This is the way we're doing it," allowing no room for flexibility, then you'll only be successful coaching a certain type of athlete, and that's a big mistake. One size definitely does not fit all. Every athlete is different. Some are incredibly fit while others are always on the edge of or slightly below acceptable fitness levels. Some athletes are incredibly cognizant of what's going on on the field—they see the game like the coach does—but other athletes need a lot of direction, which means you have to simplify the game for them.

If you try to coach everyone the same way, you'll wind up getting the same kind of athlete to coach, inadvertently weeding out talent that can help you win. Surprisingly, I've seen this mistake made by a lot of my players, who will dismiss potential teammates not because they don't like them, but because the prospective players don't reach the prototypical ideal of what a player "should" be. Some coaches do the same thing.

If you want successful team performance, your biggest challenge will be those players who will be the most difficult to fit into your vision of the team. These are the players who might be incredible athletes at winning on the field, but who, on a personal level, make you feel as if you're mixing oil and water. You just don't connect with them: You question their training ethics or the chemistry they have within the team, or they resist your game plan. You're going to have to decide whether or not those players should be on your team. If they make the cut, you must be flexible in the way you handle them in order to get them to buy into your team vision.

For instance, I had a player who was a member of my 1996 Olympic team. She did not fit in well with the group but had some valuable qualities that I felt could help us win the Gold Medal. In retrospect, her value was overshadowed by her shortcomings and I learned an important lesson in building a team. Your bench is a crucial source of your substitutes, but it is also a source of team support. No matter what valuable qualities she had, that player's bench personality was ultimately destructive to the team's morale.

On the other hand, remaining flexible proved to be just the right way to handle Brandi Chastain. She was cut from the team in 1991 and when she came back for a tryout in 1993, she wasn't fit enough. The next time Brandi called me was in 1995, when I was head coach. "I'm going to come back and I'm going to be fit," she told me, and she was. But even then, there were times when we would be ready to perform fitness routines and she would say, "My knee's bothering me a little, I don't know if I can go one hundred percent."

I could have said, "Brandi's below my ideal and I'm going to cut her and look for another player." But if I had done that, I would have let go one of the best players in the world, which certainly wouldn't have helped our team. Instead, I kept working with Brandi, encouraging her, letting her know when she didn't meet the standard. Eventually she got into it, and today she's one of the fittest players on the Women's National Team.

Allowing Individuality

Soccer is a game in which players express themselves personally and creatively in the way they play. If you try to make everyone play a certain way, you run the risk of losing the artistry that makes soccer and the individual player so special.

At a youth soccer game you'll probably hear parents and coaches on the sidelines yelling, "Pass the ball! Pass the ball! Pass the ball!" Well, I'm not sure a lot of people told Allen Iverson to pass the ball on the basketball court. And thank goodness they didn't, because his style of play, penetrating with the dribble and shooting or passing the ball, is his way of expressing himself. He's going to beat players to the basket or dish out a perfect pass. That's what he does best.

When we continually tell our young soccer players to pass the ball, we're not allowing them to develop their full potential, especially those who have the ability to take their opponents on and beat them one-on-one. As a result, we run the risk of diminishing a player's artistry and potential. Instead, we should teach them how to perform *all* the basics of the game, including dribbling as well as passing. It's the coach's job to create an atmosphere in which players can improvise, allowing them to take their game to a higher level.

Creating Community

Community has always been a big part of coaching. If you think back to all the great teams—the Boston Celtics, the New York Yankees, the Green Bay Packers, the Los Angeles Lakers—you'll find they created a team culture that included a sense of community.

The Women's National Team that I coached was the best example of *team* that I have ever witnessed. They were all incredibly supportive of one another. The players cared about one another's performances. They enjoyed one another's company. And perhaps most of all, they completely bought into the vision we had for the team—that we were the best team in the world and that we wanted to sustain excellence. In today's society this is a little bit more difficult to achieve, in part because people are encouraged to voice their opinions and think independently, which, as I've said before, is often a desirable quality. Nevertheless, this freedom does sometimes distract players from reaching what should be a common goal.

The job of the coach is to create a sense of unity within a team, to make sure that everyone understands what the goal is and how each player can best help the team reach it. That vision needs to be revisited frequently and made an explicit part of the team culture.

One of the unofficial programs our staff initiated was a system of big and little sisters. We tried to room veterans with younger team members as well as grouping them together during training. A wonderful example of how this worked was Joy Fawcett and Shannon MacMillan. When Shannon, who came from the University of Portland with Tiffeny Milbrett, first joined the team, Anson Dorrance was the coach, and I think she was a little intimidated by him and a number of his University of North Carolina players who were also on the team. As a result, she tended to separate herself from the group somewhat. While growing up, Shannon had a difficult family life, but she had a tremendous love of children. Joy Fawcett has two little girls, Catie and Karli, and Shannon naturally gravitated toward Joy and her family. Eventually, Joy became very close to Shannon, and because Joy was so well respected by the team, Shannon found herself more accepted by the other players. As a result of what had now become a safer environment, Shannon became more comfortable. Now she wasn't afraid to fail because she knew that even if she did, she wouldn't be ostracized. Due in large part to this newfound sense of security, Shannon developed into our leading scorer in the Olympics.

Fostering Leadership

The best teams have not just one leader but many layers of leadership. Don't misunderstand. Certainly, you need one leader to be above all other leaders, but you also need other players to fill that role when it's necessary. For instance, on the National Team, Carla Overbeck was our number-one leader, but Julie Foudy was right up there too. And then we had Michelle Akers, Kristine Lilly, Tisha Venturini, Mia Hamm, Briana Scurry, Joy Fawcett and others who at different times stepped up and took a leadership role. Incidentally, this proved to be quite an asset when they became a part of the Women's United Soccer Association (WUSA) because they were dispersed among different teams and thrown into situations where they had to be leaders on their respective teams.

Layers of leadership are important because when they're in place and the team is unified as to what the vision is—whether it be to win the Gold Medal, the World Championship, or even a girl's amateur tournament—there's no way you can lose your course. No one on the team had any problem knowing that Carla Overbeck was our number-one leader, but at various times all the other players contributed to the leadership in different ways, with different gestures, actions or words. Kristine Lilly, for example, led every single day with her commitment to excellence and the way she trained. She was a great role model for fitness and set a standard that the entire team continually strove for. Everyone knew that if you played alongside Kristine Lilly, you would be a better player for it. She would lift the level of your game, make you perform at a higher level and, as a result, you would commit more.

We often used the analogy of a flock of flying geese. After a while the lead goose has to move back—the most wear and tear is at the apex of the flight formation—and another goose takes the lead for a while, and so on.

I used a very practical exercise to foster this sense of layered leadership. By nature of their position on the field, goalkeepers have to have significant leadership skills. So I would say to them, "Each of you take half the team. I want you to warm them up, and

I'll give you ten minutes before meeting back here." Another technique is to assign players to organize their own teams. By delegating authority you're reinforcing the sense of leadership, while giving different players the opportunity to lead. I'd often say, "Okay, Joy, we're playing 6v6.* You organize your team over here. Tiffeny, you organize your team over there. I'll give you one or two minutes together and then we'll play." By not always choosing the same two people to lead, you're giving everyone a chance to practice leadership skills and assume responsibility to lead the team. Some players are so intimidated with the responsibility of leadership that even a simple exercise like this creates tremendous anxiety. By carefully observing and giving appropriate feedback, a coach or parent can assist the "assuming of leadership" process.

Although, as I've said before, there has to be one overall charismatic leader, sometimes the coach doesn't have total control over who that leader will be. You always hope it's a positive leader. And if it's not, you have to work with other members of the team to reinforce the positive vision you want to create, or consider replacing the leader. I've seen a lot of leaders who are negative. They do things that undermine the team's performance. They can also create dissension within the team, which obviously eats away at any success you might have, and they make it impossible to create a united community. Gradually, with care and patience, the goal to transform that initially negative leader into a positive model of individual and team commitment can succeed.

Teaching Tolerance

Tolerance is important not only between and among teammates but also for individual players personally. Ideally, this tolerance starts at the top with the coach. Players make mistakes, some of them physical and some mental. It's the job of a coach to point out those mistakes, to help each player recognize the error and then, more important, provide the tools to correct it. It's also the job of the coach to make it clear that if a player makes a mistake, it's not the

---

*Six versus six; this kind of abbreviation appears throughout text.

end of the world. It's equally vital to coach players when they've been successful. In fact, the most enlightened coaches spend more time congratulating successes than correcting mistakes.

Over the years I've had players who, when they made a mistake, were clearly much harder on themselves than they would have been on a teammate who'd made the same mistake. These players take themselves down emotionally and tear themselves up mentally. Frankly, I was like that too. But what you have to understand is that if you're a member of a team, you have the responsibility to keep your own performance up. If you tear yourself down or beat yourself up, you're not only hurting your own performance but also the collective performance of the team.

It's crucial to teach your players to have tolerance for their own performance and a realistic understanding that no one's perfect. Obviously, this isn't easy for most of us. To facilitate the process you can encourage your players to begin to build in key words or phrases that will get them back on focus. As a goalkeeper I used to say to myself when I'd make a mistake in a game, "Okay, that was a bad play, but you're going to need to come up with a big play to win this game." So immediately, instead of focusing on the bad play I'd just made, I started focusing on that big play in order to reshape my mental approach. I didn't know when I was going to make it, but I knew that when I got the opportunity, it was going to be a big play that would turn the game around. In essence, my focus shifted from the past to the present because I needed to be ready now, in the moment.

Besides teaching self-tolerance, a coach must insist that his or her players are tolerant of their teammates. You cannot have a successful team if you have players who, when somebody makes a mistake, point fingers at their teammate or exhibit body language that says, "What the hell is this person doing?" This kind of behavior definitely does not help performance. Instead, you need leaders and teammates who will actively support each other and boost the team's competitive edge through their understanding of competitive dynamics. The best example I've ever seen of this occurred during the quarterfinals of the 1999 World Cup. We were playing Germany, one of the best teams in the world, and in the first five minutes of the game, Brandi Chastain kicked the ball into our own goal (essentially scoring a goal for Germany). She was in shock. At that point Carla Overbeck came up to her and said, "Brandi, we've got eighty-five minutes left to go. We'll get the goal back. But we need you in the game. Let's play."

This snapped Brandi back into the moment. The fairy-tale ending is that Brandi actually ended up scoring the tying goal in the second half of that World Cup quarterfinal. I don't think she would have scored that goal without the support and tolerance of her teammates for a very unfortunate mistake at a very crucial point in the game.

On a personal level, an individual has to be pretty courageous to stay in there physically and emotionally to turn things around. It's not an easy thing to do when a player's confidence is in the gutter. Some can do it consistently, but other players can only do it occasionally. I think it's the coach's job to try to facilitate the likelihood of that happening. You have to trust your players, trust that they can turn things around, trust that they can overcome their mistakes, and believe that they will be successful. If you must take a player out of the game, and sometimes you will, then you've got to build up that player's confidence as soon as possible. In essence, you've got to rebuild her self-esteem. Players need to know that your coaching decisions are performance related and not personal. Colleen had some great advice for helping players to do that. She would tell the players, "Look, let's get past it now. Let's focus on the plays you know you *can* make and *have* made so well and so often in the past. Let's play in the moment and deal with the mistakes later."

Any coach knows that winning is much more than simply having great talent, although that certainly helps. Success is also a matter of coaching style and the kind of relationship you have with your players and they have with each other. I believe that fostering the new model of the champion by incorporating a much more humanistic approach to coaching will result in having fun and a winning season.

CHAPTER 3

Coaching the Young Athlete

If it isn't fun, it's not soccer.
— Tony DiCicco

The last thing my players on the Women's National Team saw before they left the locker room was a sign that read, PLAY HARD. PLAY
TO WIN. HAVE FUN. Coaches have always stressed playing hard and
playing to win, but it's surprising how often they take the fun out of
training and out of games. If you do that, you're clearly affecting
performance as well as risking the chance that your players will not
learn to love and appreciate the game. And with young athletes,
anywhere from six to eighteen years old, there's one thing that must
be consistent in playing soccer—or any other sport, for that matter:
It's got to be fun.

    In addition to the elements necessary for any successful coach—
a knowledge of the game, patience and communication skills—
coaching young players also has its own set of requirements. Here
are some of the principles you can use:

Fitness and Training

Too many coaches of young athletes are obsessed with fitness but,
in fact, for children under the age of twelve there are very few advantages to separate fitness training. Instead, fitness is the game

itself, playing with the ball or creating imaginative exercises that keep young players from getting bored and turning away from the game. When coaching younger players you ought never say, "Okay, put the balls away and let's *run*." That doesn't work. Young players need efficient, economic training that incorporates fitness into the actual learning and practicing of the skills required to play the game. You can play games with the ball that are demanding and fun. Whether it's 1v1, or keep away with the ball, you can teach the skills of the game, the psychological tactics and the drive to win against all odds as well as provide fitness training.

With teenagers you can begin to introduce more traditional fitness methods. There are, for instance, particular demands of the game you probably want to work on because now you're training specific movements and physical abilities. In some cases, you are going to have your players do separate fitness routines that may or may not include the ball. Still, I'd stress keeping it very light, perhaps only 5 percent and certainly no more than 10 percent of your training time. Practice should still be with the ball 90 percent of the time, some of which will obviously include fitness training.

With the Women's National Team we spent perhaps one hour without the ball for every ten hours of training. I see too many coaches of younger athletes presenting fitness training to their players well in excess of the 10 percent threshold. I think this is a mistake because the game is not simply a matter of running but of using the ball with confidence, poise and skill. My experience is that most coaches of elite teams feel that the most underdeveloped area among players is their technical ability or individual skill level with the ball.

Over the years, I've coached my sons at ages six, seven and eight, and I know that for younger children training sessions need to be no longer than an hour. The activities also need to be varied and short. In other words, you don't try to train a group of seven year olds for an hour using only two or three different drills or practice exercises. Instead, you should have the players do six or eight different exercises: They're in one and then they're out of it, they're in another one, then they're out of it. You know you're doing a good job if the kids are saying, "Can we play this longer?"

And if that does happen, you should say, "No. That's a great exercise and we're going to do it again later, but let's do this next one now." Always try to complete a training exercise at the peak of player intensity, enjoyment and competition rather than play it out to the point of boredom or fatigue.

Teaching the Game

Coaches spend an awful lot of time teaching tactics, often telling players, for instance, that they need to stay in their positions. But what's sometimes lost is the fact that soccer is a free-flowing expression of how you want to see the game unfold. As a coach, clearly you need to keep helping players understand positioning and spatial awareness. But the last thing you want to do is lock players into specific and rigid roles by saying, "You stay here and you stay there." That's not the way the game ought to be played.

For instance, one thing I hate to see in training is a long line of girls waiting for their turn to go through a maze to practice dribbling. This methodology is totally unnecessary because players can do all the dribbling they need through free movement, where everybody's learning to be aware of space by being creative and improvising. That's how the actual game of soccer is played.

There are, however, specific activities I'd suggest as teaching tools. You can teach passing, for instance, by having the kids stand and pass the ball back and forth, but it's going to get pretty boring for them rather quickly. Instead, you can say, "Okay, here's the game. We're going to see how many passes you can get back and forth between you and your teammate in thirty seconds. You're going to keep your own score. I expect everybody to be honest with the score and if the ball goes wild, you've got to go get it together and continue playing from your new location."

What you've done is set up a competition and it becomes fun. There's also a little bit of intensity and an urgency to their play. It's not just a boring drill, it's now a competition. And to spice it up a little, don't always make it a matter of the girls competing against each other. Sometimes you can have them compete against the previous highest score, the coach, or even the scores of their parents.

Strategy

With young children, strategy and the tactics of the game will come later rather than sooner. My youngest son, who's ten years old, is playing 11v11 soccer now, and his coaches asked me to have a chalk talk with them. As we talked about what systems of play I might share with the team, I said, "At this age group, you're really teaching technique rather than strategy. It may cost you some games in terms of wins and losses, but right now it's better to teach the techniques of the game much more often than putting them out on the field and telling them where to run and when to run there. Anyone can teach tactics. But you can't learn technique overnight."

Injuries

Injuries are inherent to sports. There are very few players, with the exception of an iron man like Cal Ripken, who can compete for long periods of time without having to deal with injuries. I believe that coaches and parents should convey to their child or player that taking care of themselves is crucial. It's a fact of life that sometimes an athlete may have to play hurt—perhaps she was kneed in the calf or scraped her knee—but we never want her to play injured. If a player runs the risk of further or long-term physical damage, the player should not play. This is an important distinction for coaches and parents to make. What parent hasn't had a child who, no matter how seriously she's injured herself, wants to get right back into the game? But that's not always the prudent or safe thing to do. And you can't leave that decision up to the child. It's your job as a coach or parent to make the call, and sometimes it's a tough and unpopular decision.

I don't know of any top athletes who can completely and accurately give themselves the therapy they need. This is especially true at the youth level, where there will not be trainers and doctors on the field. So, for example, if one of your players sprains an ankle, what are you going to do?

When an ankle is sprained, it starts bleeding in the joint. Eventually, the bleeding will stop, but there will be swelling that will slow down the healing process. To combat this, the first thing to do with any kind of sprain is to take the athlete out of the lineup (rest) and apply ice as quickly as possible to the affected area (ice). Put the ice in a Ziploc bag or use an ice pack, then wrap it around the area or use a compression bandage (compression) to hold it in place for approximately twenty minutes with the ankle elevated (elevation). This allows the blood to flow away from the area, which also slows the swelling process. Use the ice for twenty minutes every hour. Once the ankle is feeling better, heat can be applied, but remember, even by just walking around, the athlete is bringing heat to the area, so when she stops, reapply ice. The common acronym for this entire first aid process is RICE, for rest, ice, compression, elevation.

Sometimes injuries are far more serious than they appear and may have grave, career-ending consequences. Other times, through sheer willpower and dedication, players can make remarkable comebacks from potentially devastating injuries. Danielle Fotopoulos, the all-time collegiate leading scorer, the same player who broke Mia Hamm's and Tiffeny Milbrett's records, tore her ACL (anterior cruciate ligament) during training camp in 1997. This injury required surgery and nine months of rehabilitation. Not only did Danielle come back, she made the World Cup Championship Team in 1999. Similarly, Brandi Chastain had two separate knee and ACL injuries, and she, too, made a successful recovery. But the quickest recovery from a serious injury that I ever witnessed with a soccer player was when Amanda Cromwell suffered an ACL injury on February 17, 1996, and competed for a position on the Olympic Team on May 20. It was a remarkable recovery because Amanda put so much time and effort into rehabilitation. Her commitment paid off: She made the Olympic Team as a reserve.

Kept in perspective, there may even be silver linings in having an injury. One is the appreciation a player develops for her sport. Sometimes, she doesn't realize how important soccer is until it's taken away. Facing the risk of losing forever the opportunity to play serves as potent motivation for many athletes. Another is that when a player undergoes a serious injury requiring rehabilitation, she is put on a routine in the weight room along with other reconditioning activities. Often the injured athlete becomes so dedicated to weight training that she comes back stronger than ever. And by the time she does come back, weight training has become an integral part of her everyday life.

Often players do not take enough time to recover and, in the long run, that makes the recovery process even longer. On the other hand, sometimes parents may be too conservative, keeping their daughters out too long. It's natural for parents to worry about their children—we all do—and yet I think we have to be careful not to baby them too much. I had a rule with my wife when our sons were young and they would fall on the athletic field with what appeared to be an injury. The rule was *You can never go onto the field unless it appears to be very serious.* The reason for this is that some of the worst scenes I saw when I coached children were when a mother or father would come running from the stands and onto the field. It's best to leave the intervention to the coaches. I know that's a tough call, but I believe that at some level we have to begin building toughness into our sons and daughters so they understand that on occasion they're going to play with a few bumps and bruises. This teaches them, among other things, that they can get from point A to point B without all of their faculties, that they may have to be a little bit smarter, or if they can't run quite as fast, they need to learn how to be successful in a different way. Players also learn that they can survive on their own. Besides, most kids would be terribly embarrassed having Mom or Dad come out on the field to rub that sore spot in front of their teammates, coaches and fans.

Winning . . . and Losing

In our society, winning is often looked at as the most important thing and, I think, for the most part that's fine. Often the first question we ask our children after a game is, "How'd you do?" What we are really asking is, "Did you win or lose?" But sometimes we need to curb that attitude because all too often winning becomes the dominant factor in what we do. Certainly, as players get older and the stakes get higher, winning plays a larger role. Yet winning should never be the sole criterion for success because winning or losing often comes down to a referee's decision, one key play in the game or even luck. In other words, as players we cannot always directly control who wins. But, and this is the key distinction, we can determine how we play, how we train and how we interact with our teammates, our opponents and the referees. For instance, when we were in Sweden playing Denmark for the 1995 World Cup, Briana Scurry was red carded, which meant she would have to sit out the next game. Believe it or not, I had to put Mia Hamm in as goalkeeper to finish out the game—and we won. When asked about it in a press conference afterward, I said, "I would hate to be judged on one game as a player or coach and I'm not going to judge this referee based on one game either."

Before your season begins, you should establish the goal that would constitute success and victory for you and your team. This might not be the obvious ultimate prize, like winning a championship. Instead, it might be bettering the previous year's record, or finishing over .500 or finishing in the top half of the division. The goal then becomes the objective for which to strive. This will be the criterion that will determine if your team was successful, not their record. When people ask me about the Olympics in 1996 or the Women's World Cup in 1999, I remember more than winning the Gold Medal. My favorite memories are of the time spent on the training field with my players, our ups and downs and how together we molded the team into something special. In fact, it was the journey to the Olympics and the World Cup that were my favorite times as head coach of the Women's National Team.

Parental Guidelines

Parents are one of a coach's best assets, but they can also be one of the biggest challenges. In order to get the best from them, a coach must create guidelines, just as he or she does with players. It's also a good idea to occasionally meet after games with the parents as a group to discuss the upcoming schedule or to commend them or even challenge them to higher conduct if the situation warrants.

• Officiating

At the youth level, most officials are inexperienced. They make mistakes and they miss calls. Nevertheless, you must set down the rule to your players and to their parents that no matter what, no one yells at the officials. There are two good reasons for this: You don't want your players to assume that every time they're beaten it's because of the referees, and you want to foster good sportsmanship. Nonetheless, inevitably someone—the coach, parent or player—will argue a call. The key is to bring everyone back into the established team standard when the rule concerning referees is broken.

• Cheering

Another essential rule is that both as coaches and as parents we should not yell at our players. We can encourage them, but should not chastise them because they've failed. I've always told parents that if they want to understand how difficult it is to play the game of soccer, they should bring a pair of cleats to one of our practices and get out there on the field. When they do, they'll see that the ball just doesn't always do what you expect or want it to.

I recall sitting down with parents and asking, "What do you want from your child this season?" The answers ranged from "I want her to enjoy being part of the team" or "I want her to develop an appreciation of physical activity" to "I want her to develop some skills and some aggressiveness." No matter what reasons were given, my answer was always the same: "We can accomplish all those things, but if you want your child to win every game, that's not my goal here. My goal is to encourage and develop the players so that they love this game and are able to play it a long time. Certainly we want to win, but it's not a win-at-all-costs scenario." Winning, at the younger youth levels, should be way down near the bottom of the priority scale. Once you get parents to identify what they really want for their children, they will help each other stay in line.

• Parental Cooperation

When I was coaching kids, the parents used to show up for practice and they'd bring their chairs and they'd sit down and watch. It didn't take me long to recognize that a very valuable asset was going to waste. So I'd say to them, "Hey, next practice bring your sneakers because we're all coming out here to play." The next time they came out, I'd have the parents be monsters and we'd play monster tag, in which the kids would dribble their soccer balls, changing directions, trying to escape their parents. By facilitating interaction in this way, you'll not only teach skills, but you'll also nurture the relationship between moms and dads and their kids, allowing them to enjoy and appreciate the game of soccer together.

• Dealing with Intrusive Parents

At every competitive level I've had experience with parents who were too intrusive. Generally, I think you have to give them their say, allowing them the same kind of empowerment you give your players. Sometimes you'll agree with what they have to say and sometimes you won't, but listening to them is a start, even if, in the end, you have to agree to disagree.

Parents often have unrealistic aspirations for their children. They frequently want them to compete at a level they aren't prepared for, at least in terms of experiencing success. If this happens, you have to pull them aside and say, "Your child is a wonderful athlete, but right now the best thing for her is to just enjoy the game and play in her own age group." Of course, there may be a situation when playing up at an older age group is also the right choice for that particular player. The decision must be made on an individual basis. Placing each player in a competitive situation in which she can be optimally challenged and experience success is the key goal.

Understand that you're not going to get through to every parent. Some are going to buy into what you have to say and others aren't. One of the things you can do to help facilitate your connection with parents is to have a parent liaison work with you, not only assisting you administratively, but also helping you communicate with the other parents. Conducting team meetings with the parents and providing written guidelines of your goals and expectations for players and parents will also facilitate a positive experience for everyone involved.

• Coaching Your Own Children

Some of the most rewarding experiences I have ever had as a coach were with my own sons and seeing them emerge as competitors, teammates, athletes and fine young men. I know something about parents coaching their own children because I've done it and have made every possible mistake. Just recently one of my sons, who's a junior in high school, was having a captain's practice and I said to him, "Would you like me to come over and run practice?"

"No, that's okay, Dad," he said, "we're all set."

After he left I said to my wife, "I could have gone over and run his practice."

"Tony," she said, trying to set me straight, "he doesn't look at you and see the Olympic coach. He looks at you and sees 'Dad,' and he didn't want his dad to run *his* practice."

Earlier, one of my other sons, Andrew, had trouble being coached by me because he took it very personally, not as coach to player but as father to son. Much later I was playing basketball with him, my other sons Anthony and Alex and my youngest son, Nick. At one point I turned to Nick, who was my teammate, and said to him, "Do it this way." He burst into tears and left the court. I looked at Andrew and said, "Did you see that? That's you. That's how you respond." In that instant he got it. He saw that I wasn't being unfair to Nick, that I was just trying to coach him a little bit. But because it was his dad coaching him, he struggled with it. As a result, Andrew suddenly understood the dynamic, and since then I've been able to coach him a lot better. He's been much more open to my teaching because he's been able to listen. He understands that I'm not Dad when I'm out there on the field or on the court—I'm his coach. He understands that I am not attacking him personally but simply pointing out another way to try a particular play and be successful.

Clearly, coaching your son or daughter isn't easy. If you are able to find an appropriate balance between encouragement and pressure, however, it can be a wonderfully rewarding experience. What you must understand is that no matter what you say and no matter how you say it, it often registers as a personal attack when it comes from dad or mom. It's important to explain that to your child—that this is not coming from dad or mom; it's coming from the coach. You must also recognize that you're likely to be harder on your own child than you are on the other players and deal with it accordingly.

Don't be afraid to praise your child. If you let your daughter know when things aren't happening the way they should, then make sure you hit the high notes as well. Acknowledge her strengths and accomplishments at every opportunity. Not long ago I ran the school practice for two of my sons, and I made sure both of them heard a lot of praise. I must have done all right because when I got home later that night my older son came up to me and gave me a pat on the back, which I think signified thanks for helping out.

Frankly, I don't think it's a great idea to discuss sensitive game situations with your child once you're off the field, but if you have a relationship where you can do that, just make sure you don't overdo it. It's taken me a long time to be able to get to that point, but I've learned to be as nonjudgmental as possible. But no matter what, understand that there are going to be some difficult moments and that, in the end, it is often better to coach less than more.

When it comes to coaching a youngster, the bottom line should always be that the child have fun. If your daughter comes home, goes to the backyard and starts kicking the ball around, you know that the coach has done a great job. On the other hand, if she comes home and throws the ball into the garage and doesn't take it out again until she goes to practice, then there's a good chance that she's not benefiting from a motivational and rewarding coach.

COLLEEN'S TEAM-BUILDING EXERCISES*

Icebreakers

Like any good practice session, team building should begin with a proper warm-up to prepare athletes for the day's events. Warm-up activities can be thought of as simple icebreaker experiences to encourage athletes to make the transition from the physical, competitive mode to a more relaxed and open spirit of engagement.

Games in which inhibitions are lessened and activities where individuals can get to know one another, have fun and take some personal risks are called icebreakers. As the saying goes, "You never get a second chance to make a first impression." This is certainly applicable to successful team building. Start with a bang. Make the activity an attention grabber that leads and motivates the group into the rest of the day's activities. Begin with a high-energy, engaging initiative that immediately captures the attention of the participants. An exciting beginning can serve as a bridge from the current to the next level of involvement and sets the tone for future challenges. Here is one example of a simple icebreaker. It incorporates competition, problem solving and communication.

Laying the Ground Rules
Whenever you introduce an exercise, you should give the team ground rules, including the goals for the activity and any team rules you want to encourage—for example, "Only positive verbal comments are to be shared," "Let's all respect individual differences" or "Let's foster a safe environment both physically and emotionally."

---

*Many of these team-building activities are modified or refined versions of initiatives and games by Karl Rohnke and Steve Butler as contained in *QuickSilver* (1995), *Silver Bullets* (1984), and *Cowtails and Cobras II* (1989), all published by Kendall/Hunter Publishing Company, and Terry Orlick's *The Cooperative Sport and Games Book* (Pantheon Books, 1978).

Let players know that while they may be having a great time laughing, having fun and enjoying themselves, there is a deeper meaning embedded in these games that will be explored later in the day.

Debriefing

Many team leaders commit the error of focusing almost exclusively on the initiatives themselves and neglecting the debriefing session at the end of practice when lessons extracted from the day's activities should be explored with the entire group. Players' opinions should then be drawn out, and they should be asked to explain what they saw, heard, learned and felt during the team-building activities and what potential applications could be derived for the team or for the season. In many ways, the debriefing sessions are as important, if not more so, than the activities themselves. With experience, team leaders will increase their skills in both the art and science of leading activities and in discussing their use, value and application for the team.

Ongoing Follow-up

Finally, it is essential that coaches continue to highlight the themes revealed in the team-building sessions in subsequent practice sessions on the field. In other words, the lessons should be revisited throughout the year and not simply left at the site of the team-building activities.

Knock Knock! Who's There?

Objective

To bring a collection of individuals together in the first effort of forming a new group in a nonthreatening, fun way.

Equipment

You will only need a blanket, sheet or very large towel.

Space

Minimal

Number of Players

Divide your entire group into an even number of teams (either two, four, six or eight equal teams). It is best to have two teams of at least six players each.

The Game

Have each team sit on the floor facing each other while two team leaders, managers or coaches stand in the middle holding up the blanket, sheet or towel so that neither team can peek over, under or around the barrier to see the other team.

Ask one player from each team to sit closer to the divider (blanket or sheet), stay seated and face the divider (hence, they are closer to the other team and are facing their "opponents"). These opponents are still completely prohibited from seeing one another and are still separated by the barrier.

On the count of three or following the command "Knock knock! Who's there?" both leaders holding the blanket or sheet drop the barrier in one quick releasing motion.

At that moment both competitors facing each other can see one another and should shout, out loud (and instantaneously), their opponent's name.

Whoever shouts the correct opponent's name first wins that round and the "loser" (whose name was called first) now switches over and joins the other team.

The game continues until one team has successfully captured everyone but one member of their opponent's team.

Variation

Same game but now the players call out their opponent's last name. Or each player could call out their opponent's position on the team.

Debriefing

Why is this exercise important?

What does it accomplish?

What did you notice about your speed of thought when you got excited in the game or when you were competing in the game?

How did this exercise help in getting to know your teammates?

TONY'S CHALK TALK

Aerobic Fitness

There are two types of physical fitness—aerobic and anaerobic. Aerobic fitness is exercise that can be sustained over a long period of time while anaerobic training, which lasts a short time and is of high intensity, involves maximum effort from 0 to 12 seconds. Soccer athletes must have a solid aerobic base prior to layering in their anaerobic fitness.

Here are some options for aerobic fitness.

Option 1 Cones

Starting from the end line but not within the goal area, place a row of cones 5, 10, 15, 20 and 25 yards out. Have your players run first to the 5-yard cone and back, then to the 10-yard cone and back and so on until they finish the course, at which time they will have run a total of 150 yards.

The time to complete one cycle varies depending on the age of your players. The Women's National Team completed the 150-yard course in 35 seconds, which, for them, was about a 70 percent sprint. The players would then have the remainder of the minute, about 25 seconds, to rest before starting again until they had completed 10 rounds of this exercise. If you have teenage athletes participating at a moderate ability level, I would suggest starting at 40 seconds to complete the course and 40 seconds to rest before repeating it. Repeat 4 times and work up to 8, then reduce the rest period to 30 seconds.

Remember, for athletes younger than twelve, there is no need to do any fitness without the ball, so I would suggest introducing the same exercise using a ball, which they dribble to each cone and back. Obviously, with younger athletes the time frame will have to be adjusted accordingly. Repeat 4 times with a 60-second rest between cycles. For older athletes it may be useful to do one cycle without the ball, then one with it, comparing the two cycles to see how close they get their dribbling the ball time to their running time.

Option 2: Stinkers

Starting at the end line, players must run to midfield and back 3 times. Total distance depends on the length of the field, but will probably be between 300 yards to 360 yards. The standard time for the Women's National Team was either 60 seconds with a 60-second rest or 65 seconds with a 45-second rest. As better fitness is attained, I would reduce the rest time. The Women's National Team would repeat this exercise up to 10 times, but obviously with younger athletes this would be excessive. This exercise can also be done with a ball; just modify the time required to finish and cut down on the overall distance.

For very young athletes or beginner players, this aerobic exercise must be done with very few repetitions but with adequate rest. I would suggest giving 90 seconds to finish with 60-second rests. Start with 3 reps and build to 6 reps.

Option 3: Team Escort Run

This exercise, which can be performed with or without a ball, can be a competition rather than pegged to a time standard.

First, divide your team into groups of three or four. Runner 1 runs a designated distance (20 yards work well) and back. When she gets back, runner 2 joins her and they both go (runner 2 could dribble a ball up and back). When they return, runner 2 drops off and runner 3 runs with runner 1 (or dribbles a ball as runner 1 runs). When they return, runner 4 takes runner 1 out and back. Now it's runner 2's turn to be escorted out and back with her teammates.

The Women's National Team loved this type of fitness because it also served as a team-building exercise.

Questions and Comments

How often should you do aerobic fitness?

It depends on where you are in your season and the tolerance levels of your players. With the Women's National Team, I did not do fitness training more than 3 times per week in the preseason and not more than once or twice a week, depending on the game schedule, during the season. If you do fitness every day, you may think you will end up with the fittest team, but instead you will probably end up with the most injured and burned-out team.

When should you start anaerobic training?

Your players need a solid aerobic base before the benefits of anaerobic training will be maximized. Remember, however, that when you play 1v1 you are doing anaerobic training.

Coaching Challenge

How much fitness can you incorporate into your training without doing separate running sessions?

If you use short-sided games including 1v1, 2v2 and 4v4 and encourage your players to go after it, then you are doing fitness work and at the same time developing your team as soccer players.

CHAPTER 4

Tryouts: Creating Your Team

To some, challenges are exhausting. To others, they are opportunities in waiting.

—Tony DiCicco

Team tryouts can be an exciting yet stressful time for parents, coaches and kids. It's a time of great hope and disappointment. It's also the first chance a coach gets to see the players who might make up his or her team.

When we held open tryouts for the WUSA in 2000, close to two hundred women showed up, many of them at different skill levels. The coaches decided which candidates could play on their teams and, on a somewhat larger scale, which ones were qualified to play in the league. Without a plan, an idea of what they needed, it would have been a hopeless task. The same thing applies to amateur soccer, whether you're talking about kids or young adults. Preparation is the key, and listed here are a few preliminary steps coaches can take to make the process a little easier.

1. Make a plan. Decide what you're trying to accomplish and how you're going to accomplish it. How many spots are there on the team? What kinds of players do you want? How are you going to judge players' skills?
2. Make sure you have the proper equipment, space and resources to get the tryouts done efficiently.

3. Make sure this is as gentle a process as possible, especially if you are working with younger kids, whose egos can be rather fragile.
4. Encourage parents to attend tryouts. They can be a valuable resource. I would let them know beforehand what the procedure is going to be so that there are no surprises.
5. If it's feasible, bring in a couple of other volunteer coaches to help you. The reason is simple: You may already know a lot about these players, but another coach may see something totally different in a player that you're not able to see. Also, because it's the first day, the volume of potential players will be high and it will be difficult for you to handle them alone.
6. As a coach, you might have a different experience with girls at tryouts. Girls often have less of a personal history and less of an indoctrination into sports culture than boys and their parents may not have provided them with important information about the tryout process. As a result, you may have to spend a little more time going over the basic rules of the game and how tryouts work.
7. Don't let the session run too long. You don't need tryouts to be so drawn out that you prolong the heightened level of anxiety for athletes. For the youngest age group, I would make the session no longer than an hour. As you progress to the older athletes, eleven and up, you can train as long as an hour and a half.

Preparing Your Child for Tryouts

How much you can help prepare your child for tryouts depends, in part, on what level they're playing. The first thing I think a parent should do to help their child is be honest. One of my sons plays for the Region 1 Olympic Development Team at the under-seventeen level, and he was headed down to Florida to try out for the Youth National Team. He has some unbelievable strengths in his game, but he also has some areas that need improvement to enable him to become a complete player. So the first thing I wanted to do with him was to make sure I was very positive with my feedback. I told him all the things he does very well and then I told him which area he had to be conscious about improving. I was able to sit with him and say, "If I were a National Team coach and I saw you play and do this, this and this, I'd probably eliminate you from the competition, and here's why . . ." Next, I offered suggestions about how he could make some of the changes necessary to improve that particular aspect of his performance. Then I finished with a couple of important positive traits that he has in his game.

Boys and girls often get advice from their parents about sports, especially from their fathers. But it might not be as simple for fathers to make the correlation between what their experience was like growing up and trying out and what their daughters' experiences will be. Nevertheless, I think it's very important for fathers and mothers to share their sports experiences with their daughters (and their sons). Men may feel a greater obligation to prepare their sons for competition, but they also have to prepare their daughters. If they don't do it, then it's up to others in the family, school or community to take on that role.

I remember a great Hallmark card TV commercial featuring a young figure skater, aged twelve or thirteen. Her mother says to her, "I have two cards for you, one if you win and one if you don't." The girl opens up the first card and it reads, "I love you. Mom." Then she opens up the second card, and it contains the exact same message. This is how I believe you should deal with your children. You can't judge them by what they do on the field because they may learn to equate your love and approval with their performance in sport. Just because they may not exhibit the effort or interest we might prefer doesn't mean we ought to use that fact to judge them as human beings. It's possible that soccer may not be the thing that gets their competitive juices going, and that's okay.

Here are some tips parents can use to prepare their daughters for tryouts.

- Remind them that every coach responds to the first player running in from the field after being called. It shows that you're eager to learn. As a coach, you're always aware of the players who hustle, who show enthusiasm. By the same token, you always recognize the player who's the last one out on the field or the player who seems lethargic and unenthusiastic.

- Talk with your daughter. Ask her what she thinks her best position is and what her strengths are. Then offer your opinion and ask what the coach thinks.
- Take your daughter out to the park or the backyard and practice with her before the tryouts. When my sons were going through this process, I used to take them down to the soccer fields on a Saturday and go through a few things that were relevant to the position they wanted to play. Obviously I have a bit of an advantage over most parents, but there's no reason why you can't try it too.
- Give them contingent, constructive and positive feedback and offer encouragement. Try to make them feel good about themselves and the sport.
- Stress the fun part of tryouts. "Just go out there and have fun and show them what you can do" is what you ought to be telling them.
- Help them understand that no one play is going to put them on the team, nor is one play going to take them off the team. This advice will help take off some of the pressure.

The Welcoming

When I was holding tryouts at the younger levels, I would first bring the parents and children in together. I'd have the children sit down with their parents standing behind them and I'd say, "Look, this is a tryout, which means that not everyone is going to make *this* team. We are planning, however, if there is enough interest in having a second team, to have a B team that will play a game schedule and be a lot of fun."

It's also a good idea to tell them that there is a mechanism for moving from one squad to another and then explain to them what that process is. You've got to be up front with them so they know that it's not the end of the world if they don't make this particular team. In fact, you can tell them the true story about the legendary Michael Jordan, who was cut from a basketball team when he was young—and he's gone on to win numerous NBA titles and league MVP honors. You might want to share a personal anecdote as well.

For example, I was cut from my seventh-grade soccer team and was somehow able to overcome the initial disappointment, eventually becoming a professional player and coach. Your final word might be something like, "Part of growing up is learning how to deal with disappointment, but in the meantime, let's just have some fun!"

Getting Started

When you're dealing with kids, the most important ingredient for a successful practice is to keep them active. It's a big mistake to say things like, "Stand over there, your turn's coming up." Keep them moving. Keep them entertained. The goal is to achieve maximum participation for a maximum number of players for the greatest amount of time. Besides, the best way to evaluate players is to see them when they're relaxed, loose, having fun and actually playing in some form of a game of soccer. These games also act as great ice-breakers. They loosen up the players, allowing them to get several touches on the ball, and lessen the pressure and intimidation of the tryout experience. For instance, you can play short-sided games like 4v4, 5v5 or even 2v2. And don't be afraid to play 1v1. It will tell you a lot about a player's skill level and her commitment. Make sure the warm-up is varied and fun. Remember, you know you're doing a good job if you see the players smiling during warm-ups.

Putting Your Team Together

Putting together a team is like fitting together a puzzle. If you simply look for the most athletic players, you may miss creative or unique athletic genius in a player. Or if you look for just the most skillful player, you may miss the opportunity to take a fine athletic specimen and turn her into a wonderful soccer player. In evaluating and ultimately choosing your team, I would suggest breaking the players into small groups to compete against each other. During this time

- Make sure players get frequent water breaks.
- Make sure you give them an opportunity to ask questions.

- Change the groups around so that players are competing against different players. A young player may be in a group that's too difficult for her, and moving her to another group may allow her to have more success.
- If you have a large group to deal with, it's useful to have several games going on at once. This way you can look at a smaller group and get a more accurate read of a player's ability.

The First Scrimmage

At some point you're going to have to get your players into competition and begin evaluating the talent. Until they actually compete, you can't fully judge the qualities of players. Once they start to compete, however, you'll also pick up on those athletes who have special leadership qualities. There's always that child who stands quietly on the sidelines but who, when she gets into the game, suddenly blossoms into a real competitor. That's how I was. I was personally very shy, but once I got into the game I took on a new persona and became quite outgoing. You might also have a player who has somewhat lesser skills but who suddenly becomes a dynamo on the field. Tiffany Roberts is like this. Tiff was never our most technically skilled player on the Gold Medal Olympic or the World Championship Team, and though an outstanding athlete, not our most gifted. But when it came to those who were our toughest players, those who displayed the most heart on the field, there were Michelle Akers at 5 feet 10 inches and Tiffany Roberts, a head and a half smaller. This disparity in physical stature shows that heart is not measured by the size of the body.

After you finish with the warm-up games, it's time to begin your first scrimmage. This is the first time many of these kids will compete, and coaches have to remember that especially for kids with varying skills, it can be a pressure-filled experience for them. For instance, I have a young son in the fifth grade who recently played in his first basketball game in the fifth-to-sixth-grade CYO League. He was the first sub off the bench, and when he got in there the other team began to press and he turned the ball over two or three times. He also did some pretty good things and, best of all, he never gave up. But when he came home he only remembered the negative aspects of his first real competitive basketball game and said that he didn't want to play CYO basketball anymore. It's a very competitive league, and I wish he had been able to build in some success before he was faced with an intimidating situation. As coaches, we need to remember how daunting and intimidating it can be to be tested ourselves and to imagine how difficult it is for a young athlete on her first day at tryouts. For that reason I think this first practice game of the season should be a controlled scrimmage, with the coach out on the field directing play. The idea is to show the kids that they can be successful and can play the game with developing confidence.

While the athletes were playing the small-sided games, you were trying to get them to be active, break the ice and have a chance for some fun. You weren't doing a great deal of evaluating. Now, with players on the field, you're starting to evaluate the talent. You're seeing what their skill levels are. You're watching their athleticism. You're seeing how they deal psychologically with challenges and pressure: Do they quit when things aren't going well? Do they shrivel when being chased? Do they move to a higher level when being tested and challenged? The *last* thing you should be evaluating when you're dealing with younger players is tactical awareness. With these youngsters you're much more concerned about soccer basics and about making sure they have fun. Tactics will come later.

As a coach, you can also take the opportunity during tryouts to do some fundamental teaching. You should be giving input to the girls, encouraging them, showing them the proper skills. Paint a picture by demonstrating and modeling what properly executed techniques should look like. I make a point of this because I've seen many coaches in tryout situations who don't take the opportunity to coach. Instead, they'll watch the players make the same mistakes over and over again. I always had trouble just standing passively on the sidelines and observing and not educating. I'm a teacher and a coach and if I see something awkward, I'll go over to the athlete and say, "I think there might be a better way of doing this." This technique is helpful because part of what a coach needs to evaluate is whether a player can put coaching advice into her game. The next time I see that athlete play I can evaluate whether or not she listened and was able to translate coaching points onto the field. That's the ultimate sign of a coachable athlete.

Making the Cuts

The most difficult part of coaching isn't dealing with losses, it's cutting or rejecting people for the team. It's not just a simple matter of reducing numbers, it's a matter of making decisions that in essence, short-circuit the dreams of players. I don't think there's any coach, either at the professional level or the youth recreational league in a small town, who doesn't feel the pain of not choosing someone for or cutting someone from the team.

I've gone through this possibility with my own sons. I am constantly reminding the son who is trying out for the Youth National Team that there are plenty of players on the Men's and Women's National team who never made a Youth National Team. In large part that's because as they grew older they kept developing and investing more time and effort in their game. At some point all that time and effort might pay off.

Sometimes young athletes put themselves in situations where they say, "If I don't make it today, I have no chance of ever reaching my goals." That's not true and it's up to parents and coaches to deliver that message strongly and consistently. Getting cut and having to rebound from disappointment is part of what some of the great athletes have had to deal with. In December of 1995, I cut Shannon MacMillan from the team. Shannon had won just about every award a college senior could win merely a month before, and now she felt like her soccer career was over. It was a terribly difficult decision for me and one I wasn't comfortable with. But the following month I realized I needed a striker to go with us to Brazil, so I called Shannon and asked her to join us. She said yes and went on not only to make the Olympic Team, but also to be the top scorer on our Gold Medal winning team.

If there is no soccer below the level at which you are coaching, there should not be any cuts. At the recreational level, instead of cutting, create more opportunities by adding teams, perhaps at a slightly lower level of play. Of course, there are always going to be some kids (and parents) who think they're better than they really are, that they were misjudged or that the decision was political. But the truth is, at least from my experience, that kids know who the best players are. Knowing they're still going to have a chance to play will help lessen the pain of being cut from the A squad. Kids cite having fun and getting a chance to play (rather than sitting on the bench) as two of the strongest motivations for competing in sports.

When I was cutting players from National Teams, it wasn't because they were bad players. In fact, they were often very good players. I frequently made choices because I felt there were two or three players who were better for a particular position or role on the team. There's an old saying in coaching that I've often used, "I never said I had the best eighteen players, or the best twenty players, but I absolutely had the best *team*." In the end, that's what it's all about—putting together the best possible team. Coaches have to make decisions and players and parents have to understand that putting together a team is a game of numbers, of roles, of needs and responsibilities. When someone doesn't make the squad, initially they feel hurt or even angry. It's regrettable, but understandable. Some players who are cut will use it as a source of motivation for continued practice to get good enough to eventually be on that team. Others will shy away from further evaluation and tryouts because it was such a belittling and scary experience for them. What I'd like to stress is that being cut from a team is not the end of the world, and it's not, although it may seem like it at the time, a personal attack. If parents can somehow make their children understand this fact, then it will allow them to move forward—and maybe next time they will make the team.

How to Deal with a Child Who Hasn't Made the Team

As tough as it may be for a coach to cut a player from the team, it's a lot tougher on that player and on her parents. There's no getting around the embarrassment, the emptiness, the rejection. The best thing I can suggest to parents is to offer unwavering and unconditional love and support. It may seem like it to your child, but the world hasn't ended and it's up to parents to keep the sport experience in proper perspective. If parents get upset, it will be projected onto the child, only making matters worse.

What isn't constructive is making excuses for your child by saying it was a political decision or that the coach made a poor decision (which might even be the case). If you make excuses, you're only teaching your child to deflect responsibility and discount the value of merit.

What you have to remember is that for the most part, coaches really do try to get it right. If there are twenty players on a team, odds are that practically every coach will agree on the first ten players for the team. And most coaches will agree that the next five should be on the team. But probably more coaches will disagree about the last five players chosen. Coaches have an image of what they want their team to be, and they're looking for players who can help them attain that image. As a parent, you must show love and support for your child, but that doesn't necessarily translate into judging or criticizing the coach's decision. If you do, everyone's a loser.

Coaching the Exceptional Athlete

For generations upon generations, women have been asked to fit in and to support others, not to make waves. One of the great opportunities of sports is that now we're asking just the opposite of young girls and women. We're asking them to stand out, to make a difference, to be personalities. Some young girls will develop earlier than others physically, emotionally and athletically. Perhaps they come from active, athletic families, or they have older brothers and they've played sports together. With these girls the tricky question is which group to put them in. In some instances, moving players up an age group might be good for them. Then again, it might not be. These girls might get to that higher level and, although they might survive in a more competitive environment as support players, they won't learn to be personality players. The key is to evaluate each particular child to make the best decision possible given the opportunities and the characteristics of that unique athlete. One size definitely does not fit all!

Some players are so dominant that you have to remind them again and again to work on their fundamental skills and not just be comfortable with running by, through or over their opponents simply because at this stage they can. In two or three or five years they're not going to be able to do that because athletically, technically or even tactically other players are going to catch up to them. For some of these athletes, moving them up to a higher age bracket can help them learn that they have to develop other skills than just raw speed or quickness.

I'm often asked, "Should my daughter play with the boys," or sometimes a parent proudly announces, "My daughter plays on a boys' team." I am in favor of playing on a boys' team for the most talented young girls because it will certainly challenge them. There is no way, however, that they will dominate and develop that "personality player" mindset while playing on boys' teams, especially the older boys' teams. They will develop into excellent support players and their speed of play will improve, but it will be increasingly more difficult for them to really make a difference, to take the game over, to win on their own. So my advice to parents is, if your daughters play on a boys' team, they must also play on an appropriate girls' or women's team. In the end, probably the best combination is to practice with boys and compete with girls.

COLLEEN'S TEAM-BUILDING EXERCISES

The Hula Circle

Objective
To develop competition and cooperation.

Equipment
- One Hula-Hoop for each team (if you can't find Hula-Hoops, any building supply store will have plastic tubing that can be shaped into a circle and secured with duct tape).
- A stopwatch.

Number of Players
Divide your group into the number of teams you desire with eight to fifteen individuals per team.

Space
Almost any area size will do.

The Game
Each team is asked to stand in a circle and clasp hands. That grip must not be broken. Place a Hula-Hoop on the forearm of the team captain and have her regrasp the hands of her teammates to complete the hand-in-hand closed circle. On a "ready, set, go" command, teams begin to pass the Hula-Hoop around the circle without breaking the handgrips. At the moment the coach says "Go," timing should begin. Players bend and twist their bodies through the hoop by climbing through it, ultimately getting the hoop over their heads to the other side of their bodies. The entire process repeats itself as the hoop travels from teammate to teammate around the circle as fast as possible. Keep in mind that the handgrip can never be broken. If the handgrip is broken, the Hula-

Hoop must start back at the beginning. The first team to success-fully pass the hoop around the circle without breaking grip is the winner.

Variations
Have players stand with their back toward the center circle and try again. Speed up passing by asking players to compete against the stopwatch.

Lessons
Players will discover that just because their team may be far in the lead (or behind) at one point in the contest, a few small errors (or quick recoveries) on anyone's part can lead to disaster (or success). The point is that whether you are winning or losing at any given point in the contest, it is no guarantee of the final outcome. Truly, anything is possible in sport. Teams often get the lead and relax, and the loss of focus and competitive fire can be costly.

Players learn the importance of competing against someone else (as in beating the other team) as well as the value of competing against their previous best performance (as in lowering the team's best time).

At first, players will think that winning is the only goal or that winning is when they simply beat another team. Ultimately, you want them to understand that what they initially thought was good enough, fast enough and successful enough can actually be made better and faster. It is the same principle we hope they apply to life. With planning, motivation and ingenuity they can learn skills and strategies to keep lowering their previous best time and therefore improve the overall team performance.

Debriefing
What did we learn from this exercise?

How can we do it better?

What strategies did you and your teammates use to lower your time?

Were you ever ahead and then lost the lead? How did that feel?

Were you ever behind and came back to win the game? How did that feel?

How did your teammates handle a mistake made by a member of the team?

How did you feel when you made a mistake?

How do these lessons pertain to the game of soccer?

TONY'S CHALK TALK

Exercises to Use During Tryouts

During a tryout for players at a beginning or intermediate level, it is important to see that players get a lot of ball touches as well as see them perform in a larger organization (7v7 up to 11v11). Even during tryouts I like to see some teaching taking place but remember, this is not a regular training session so don't overdo the coaching. Also, before you begin the tryout session, let the players and parents know what you're looking for as well as explaining the realities of many players trying out for just a few spots. Tryouts should last no longer than a normal training session. Don't keep players out there too long.

Option 1
After warm-ups, place the players into 4v4 teams to play on a field approximately 30 x 20 (larger if they are older teenagers) and with small goals. The simplest way to organize the teams is have all the players line up with the defenders first, then the midfielders and then the forwards. Now count off by the number of teams that is appropriate (for instance, if you've got twenty-four players, you would have six teams). In 4v4 games, there are no goalkeepers and if the ball goes over the end line, just play it with a goal kick.

Winning and losing are not a factor when players are trying out, but it's not a bad idea to keep track of the scores because you may find that one player has ended up on a lot of the winning teams. This player may have just been fortunate or she knows how to complement her teammates so that the team is better with her on it.

Option 2
Play 8v8 or 9v9 (the goalkeeper is included in these games). With this number of players you can now organize the teams into positions. For a seven-field player team the alignment can be 3–2–2

plus a goalkeeper. For the 9v9 team alignment, a midfielder or forward can be added.

Questions and Comments

How long should I stay with each game?

Each game should last no longer than 15 minutes.

What happens if the goalkeepers get no action?

Create games with fewer players and with a smaller field while still using full goals and goalkeepers. You can even use a plus player to help the attack.

Should we do any other exercises?

Yes, you can set up a simplistic 2v2 in front of the goal so that players can show off their defending or attacking. Also, with this set-up the goalkeeper will be called upon to make some plays. But remember, in this 2v2 scenario, players will need replacement relatively quickly because it will be very demanding.

Coaching Challenge

Even though this is a tryout, it can still be fun and it is the coach's job to help create a more relaxed environment so that the players are comfortable enough to play their best.

CHAPTER 5

"Chemistry" Is a Verb

Chemistry is a contribution that teammates make to each other,
but it's also something a coach can create or facilitate.

— Tony DiCicco

Putting a team together is simple, but putting together a championship team requires special contributions from every player as well as the coaching staff. Taken together, these contributions create what we call team chemistry. As you come closer to opening day, you must begin to pull your team together to create the kind of chemistry that will translate into a winning season.

The definition of chemistry is an iffy thing. People always said that our team had such great chemistry, as if chemistry were an object, a thing, something you could hold on to. As Colleen reminded us daily, "chemistry" isn't a noun, it's a verb, an action, a behavior. Each person on our team had a responsibility to actively contribute to this living entity called chemistry. A team is like a new plant. You have to water it, provide it with light and space to grow. Then you have to nurture it on a daily basis. It's active, it's personal, it's individual and it's ongoing.

Chemistry is that intangible quality existing in teams that allows them to perform at a higher level collectively than they could individually. It's a structure of support and trust within the team. It's the relationship among players, among staff and among staff and players. The ultimate goal is to create a safe environment in which neither staff nor players feel as if they're under a microscope. As a result, people aren't afraid to try new things and players can play without risk of embarrassment or fear of failure.

Chemistry alone is not enough to make you a winner, but if you have the other ingredients—talent, knowledge and competitiveness—it certainly enhances your ability to win. Clearly, teams with high levels of chemistry enjoy the game more, and the whole team experience is more rewarding and satisfying. In a highly cohesive team there's more learning taking place and there's more carryover to the rest of life. The benefits go beyond the white lines of the playing field.

Of course you can win without team chemistry: We can look back in sport history and find teams that didn't like each other and still won. I don't think, however, that without chemistry you can sustain excellence and win over time the way the Women's National Team has done. One of the key aspects of a truly cohesive team is the relative selflessness of team members. One criterion I always used to pick our players was character because recruiting a negative contributor would eventually take the team down. Players should not willfully separate themselves from the rest of the group to try to be the star, but it's something we see in sports all the time. Over the years I've made mistakes with player selection that didn't help our chemistry and ultimately it influenced our team performance negatively.

Generally speaking, I think that women and girls buy into the concept of chemistry a little more readily than do men and boys. They're able to understand the concept of selflessness more quickly because girls are still socialized to have this quality. Nevertheless, I believe chemistry is a function of team, and I don't see *team* as being male or female.

On our team we had a great example of selflessness and team chemistry demonstrated by Mia Hamm. She was and is an icon, the number-one woman in sports and the number-one soccer player in the world. Yet when people asked her about that status, she continually demurred by saying, "The team is why I've been able to score this many goals and receive this many awards. It's the team, not me. By myself I could never have done it because I really am lacking in many areas. But because I found my niche within this team, I've been able to be successful."

What a great example of chemistry at work! What a great role model for her teammates and the young emerging stars to follow.

Steps to Getting Team Chemistry

- The first step toward creating team chemistry is setting expectations. Several times throughout this book I've mentioned setting goals, creating a vision (what we want to achieve, how we want to get there), which is really setting expectations. When we set those expectations, those standards—including how the team will behave around each other—and when we strive to reach those visions or expectations, we become more complete people. For instance, in certain situations I might be moody, I might have a short fuse; but when I'm with a team, I expect more of myself and so I give more. That is what you want all of your players, their parents, and the staff to feel.

    As the leader, you have to let your team know what you expect of them. If they understand the level you expect, they will strive to obtain it. The key, however, is that the coach must model that same behavior. You really must "walk your talk" to ensure that your players do also. I don't think it was an accident that we won the Fédération Internationale de Football Association (FIFA) Fairplay Award in 1996 and were the least carded team in 1999. My expectations for the team were that we would not be carded and run the risk of sitting out games because of card accumulations.

- Congratulate, expose, celebrate and reinforce the great coachable and teachable moments of positive chemistry you see. Let me give you an example. When Tracey Leone—who is now one of our Youth National Team coaches—was a player and I was on the coaching staff of the 1991 National Team, she was interviewed and asked who her favorite teammate was. Her answer was Kristine Lilly. Well, it so happened that Kristine was the player who was keeping Tracey on the bench. Wasn't that a remarkable comment to hear? Instead of trying to put down Kristine, Tracey named her as her favorite player. Sharing this kind of thing with team members will show them how they can demonstrate self-lessness to the greater entity, and in soccer there is no greater entity than the team.

- Make new team members feel a part of the group. When new players came into our National Team, I would have individual meetings with them. I would ask, "What do you think about playing here?" They might say things like, "This is my dream" or "These players have been on posters on my bedroom wall." Then I would ask, "What do you like most about them?" They would say, "Michelle Akers is such a competitor." I'd say, "You're absolutely right, but what makes her special is the way she behaves around the team." Michelle is often the target of affectionate little jokes from her teammates, but she handles it wonderfully. She doesn't say, "Hey, I'm Michelle Akers, don't make fun of me." By relating this sort of story, you're not only introducing the new player into the team, but you're also indicating to her in an informal way the kind of behavior that you, as the coach, value and respect.

  Another thing we did on the Women's National Team to help foster chemistry was to share the load on and off the field. I knew that if we were going to win, we would all have to do our part. So many teams construct a hierarchy wherein, for instance, rookies are chosen to do day-to-day tasks like carrying equipment. That's not the way we did it on our team. Every day we posted a rotating list in the equipment room of who took what—balls, cones, water, ice—out to the field. Even if you happened to be starting that day, you were expected to shoulder the load if your name came up. This became part of our team culture, and it was an effective way to create team chemistry.

- Encourage team building and cohesiveness. We did this by creating positive group experiences that didn't have anything to do with soccer. For instance, when we were in residency training for a four-week period, the staff invited the entire team over for a spaghetti and meatball dinner at a house shared by several of the assistant coaches and, believe it or not, my father-in-law. That got the ball rolling, and the next week a couple of the players had everyone over for dinner.

At one point our cocaptain, Julie Foudy, approached me and said, "We're having these dinners, but Michelle hasn't been to one of them. Can you see if you can get her to join us?" This didn't surprise me because by nine o'clock Michelle Akers was always asleep. Sometimes, for health reasons, she would not be able to attend, and she also had to maintain a very strict diet. Nevertheless, I did speak to Michelle because I thought it was a valid request. "Michelle," I said, "why don't you see if you can join us because the rest of the team would love to see you there. You're an important part of us. Even though we have to coach you by a different set of rules because of your health requirements, we still want you to be as much a part of team activities as anyone else. I'll arrange a ride back, but I think it's a good idea for you to at least put in an appearance so the team can see you. It would mean a lot to them." Needless to say, she came to the next dinner. Everyone, including Michelle, benefited from the experience.

What to Do if Your Chemistry Starts to Break Down

There are going to be times when your team chemistry seems to be falling apart and your season seems inherently filled with potential chemistry pitfalls and land mines. Perhaps you're in the middle of a long losing streak. Perhaps certain players aren't pulling their weight in practice or in games, or one of your players is acting against the best interest of the team. If any of these things happen, bring the team together and say, "Let's revisit our goals and the way we want to interact as a team. What do we want as a team?" Without naming names, talk about the particular incidents that worry you and ask the team if these occurrences are going to help or hinder it from reaching its goals. This way you'll pull individual players and the entire team back into the vision you've established.

The reason we spent a lot of time on team chemistry in 1999

was a direct result of what I'd witnessed on the U.S. Men's National Team in 1998. It was a transitional period during which the coach kept a significant number of veterans on the team. There was a core of key starters from the previous World Cup team, but the coach was also using more of the younger players. In the end, the American team came in last out of the thirty-two teams in the World Cup tournament. Talent or tactics weren't the real problem. They were competitive in every game. They just seemed to have a run of bad luck, like hitting the post with the ball and having it bounce off the field instead of in the goal. But was it really just bad luck? I don't think so. If you took a look at the American bench you would see the veterans sitting apart from the rest of the players and the coaches. Hands were crossed on their chests, and their body language spoke volumes: *What's that player doing out there? He can't play.* That lack of support, whether they realized it or not, was partly responsible for those balls hitting the post and not going in. From that observation I realized I'd have to spend a significant amount of time establishing chemistry on our team because, in large part, I thought I might have the same situation: veterans—previous Olympic starters—now playing reserve players' roles and coming in off the bench.

I think the coach of the men's team might have made a mistake in letting things ride, hoping they'd work themselves out. They hardly ever do. And I don't believe there's any one player who is more important than the overall vision and mission you have for the team—even if it's Michael Jordan or Barry Bonds. It's better to work on chemistry early and often in order to create and maintain a cohesive vision. Some coaches wait until there are severe problems and then try to intervene with team building initiatives too late in the season.

In 1999, as we were preparing for the World Cup, we had some players who were unhappy with their playing time. Two or three players would go off into a corner and start feeding each other with complaints. Within the staff we called them the complaint sessions. A typical complaint would be, "What's Tony thinking about? You should be playing more." What these players didn't understand was that these sessions were getting them nowhere, but they were eating away at the team chemistry.

Fortunately, we were able to identify and solve the problem when I brought Colleen in. Colleen spoke to our group and used some of her team-building initiatives to bring the team together over a period of time. We were able to turn things around, but more important, to this day the greatest example of chemistry is that which was displayed by the 1999 World Cup Championship team.

A soccer team has eleven players on the field and by international rules you can have only three substitutes. Yet you have twenty players on your team, so immediately you have nine players who aren't necessarily delighted that they're not playing. Then during the game you make three substitutions and those players heading for the bench aren't incredibly excited that they're coming out of the game. And why should they be? Chances are, being starters, they're all star players. So you start out with twenty players, nine aren't happy, three more become unhappy, and potentially you'll have twelve players out of twenty who are less than thrilled with their role within the team. A lot of coaches just spend their time with their eleven starters. I've even heard coaches say, "I work with the starting team, and I have my assistant coach work with the losers." It should probably be the other way around because you can't win with just eleven players. Beyond that, no one on your team should ever be regarded as a loser. You need your entire team and that's why you must spend a lot of time with the chemistry of all the players, including those who are and those who aren't playing. Each represents a support mechanism.

Here's what I mean. Shannon MacMillan was a starter on the Olympic Gold Medal team. Shannon was our lead scorer in the Olympic Games. Yet she did not start in 1999. It would have been so easy for her to sit on the bench and question what I was doing by not putting her on the field. If she had chosen that response, it would have polarized the team and lessened our chances for success. Instead, through the work that Colleen did and what we identified with as our mission, not only did Shannon avoid that route, but she also behaved in a totally opposite manner. She was a living example of how everyone should be on the bench: supportive, clear on her role and eager to perform well when she did get the chance to play.

Shannon could come off the bench and do incredible things like scoring quick goals. She had an immediate impact in every World Cup game I put her in. Of course when she was playing like that, the media would ask her, "Shouldn't you be starting? Are you going to start the next game?" They would ask me the same questions. For me the highlight of the entire World Cup competition was when Shannon came up to me after the first-round third game in Boston against North Korea. This was the game in which she was named the MVP, having scored the winning goal and added two assists. I'll always remember her saying, "Tony, I know you're getting a lot of questions from the media about my starting in the next games. I want to play every minute, but whatever you decide, I support." What more can you ask of a player than that? That is the epitome of team chemistry.

COLLEEN'S TEAM-BUILDING EXERCISES

In sport we have a saying: One's luck, two's skill. It means that it's possible to do something well once, but the success may be due only to luck. Doing something consistently well two or three times in a row shows you have mastered the skill.

Leadership is developed when a group selects its captain and then must follow his or her commands, adjust to the needs of the group and provide initiative to solve problems. The following team-building exercise will help enhance leadership qualities in all your team members while, at the same time, show how the team must work together to prevail.

Tight Rope

Objective
To learn to pull your own weight. In line with the concept of chemistry, individual players have a responsibility to contribute to the morale and success of the group. In order to be successful in tight rope, every single member has to actively contribute to team chemistry in some way. This team-building exercise requires cooperation, give and take, intuiting needs for greater or lesser exertion of force, initiative and leadership. The challenge requires several layers of leadership. If team members try to do too much (pull too hard), the group will fail. If they don't pull their own weight (pull too lightly), the group fails.

Equipment
A strong rope approximately 1/2 to 1 inch in diameter.

Number of Players
Two teams ranging from eight to twenty-six people.

The Game
Two teams or groups line up facing each other. Each team must designate a captain who is to be the only one who can speak for the

group. Each team should line up and then sit down on the ground facing each other. The coach then places a strong rope in a straight line between them.

Each person on both teams is asked to place two hands firmly on the rope with palms facing down to the ground. Hands should be placed on the rope in an alternating fashion so that the partner across the rope should have one hand (palm down as always) in between her partner's hands. The sequence is my left hand, partner's right, then my right and my partner's left. That format continues all the way down the line.

The object of the challenge is to have two equal groups on each side of the rope pull equally on both sides in order to pull themselves up off the ground in one perfectly even motion at the exact same time.

Each captain will give the instructions to her group and will count one, two, three. On three, all players should exert the requisite force to allow the group to move up to a standing position at the exact same time. Now, repeat this sequence two more times for a total of three ups and downs.

Debriefing

What made this challenge difficult?

What contributed to team success?

How important is communication to team success?

Does just one person's performance impact the team's success? If so, how?

What happens when a group of players or one person tries to do more (or less) than others?

What is the relationship, role and responsibility of individual players to the team?

How can this exercise help team performance in the future?

TONY'S CHALK TALK

Player Positions on a Soccer Team

In the game of soccer there are different positions, but unlike most other sports these positions are interchangeable. A flank defender like Joy Fawcett assisted on the winning goal in the Olympic Gold Medal game in 1996 and scored the winning goal in the 1999 World Cup quarterfinal game. Soccer players should be soccer players, able to move from different thirds of the field into different positions while still feeling comfortable about their role on the team and in the game.

Having said all this, there are still positions in soccer and they are:

Goalkeeper
Although most coaches look for the tallest player to be the goalkeeper, the essential qualities of a goalkeeper are leadership, aggressiveness (it's always easier to teach patience rather than aggressiveness), athleticism and the ability to deal with mistakes and with goals being scored.

Defenders

Central Defenders
Central defenders are usually considered the stay-at-home defenders. They don't venture upfield as much as the other players and clearly their number-one task is to stop the opposing team's best player. Central defenders should be good organizers, good headers of the ball, have good speed and take pride in their role as stoppers.

Flank Defenders
These defenders need to have good to excellent speed. They must have the endurance to get up and down the flanks of the field. They must be able to defend individually (without cover) and must have attacking abilities.

Central Midfielders

Central midfielders are the "point guards" of the team. They are probably the best ball handlers on your team. They need to have or should be able to develop a range of play, which allows them to see the entire field from an attacking standpoint. Although they only require average speed (the center midfield is a good place to mini-mize the negative impact of slower players), quickness (speed over 5 yards and change of direction) is necessary.

Flank Midfielders

These players are similar to flank defenders but with more empha-sis on attacking abilities. They need to be fast, extremely comfort-able in the attacking third of the field, able to score goals and serve great crosses with the ball. Flank midfielders have to understand defensive techniques and have the ability to take defenders on 1v1 by dribbling by them. They need excellent stamina, because they'll be moving up and down the flanks of the field.

Forwards

Forwards need to score goals or make goals happen. They also need to have the ability to hold the ball with their back toward the goal against more than one defender. They must be proficient at dribbling and taking players on to help tear defenses apart. They should be able to score with their heads and either foot. Players who are mobile (move well when away from the ball), fast and understand tactics often make the best strikers.

Systems of Play

There are a number of systems that can help organize your team. The three following systems work well for teams learning 11v11 soccer and are used by professional teams.

4–4–2

When reading a system, always start from the defense, but do not include the goalkeeper. So a 4–4–2 means 4 defenders, 4 midfield-ers and 2 forwards. This system is very symmetrical, so that when working with the right side of the team, the left side is an exact mirror. Each side has 2 defenders, 2 midfielders and 1 forward.

3–4–3

This is a system we used in the 1996 Olympics and it works well with younger girls because there are 3 forwards. This has a positive impact on attack because the girls will not have the challenge of covering as much ground on a large soccer field or of having to rotate a third forward into attack as is required in a 4–4–2 system. This system requires tremendous work from the 2 flank midfielders.

4-3-3

This is the system we used in the 1999 World Cup and it is the one used by many of the WUSA teams. The 4–3–3 includes the benefits of a 4-defender system as well as those of the 3-forward system. The 3 midfielders are positioned centrally so the flank defender—a midfielder coming out of the center and a forward winger—shares the flank space normally played by flank midfielders.

With any system of play, coaches should evaluate talent and decide which system will work best based on the talent and athletic qualities of the players on the team. At my coaching level, I could look for players to fit a specific system that I wanted to play; you probably won't have that luxury.

Coaching Challenge

Don't overemphasize the system of play. Teach players how to play soccer and use the system to help organize them on the field. Remember, too many tactical rules and regulations on players within a particular system generally results in "paralysis by analysis."

CHAPTER 6

Eyes on the Prize

It takes courage to dream big and then to allow nothing to prevent you from realizing that dream.

— Tony DiCicco

Before starting the season, a coach must create and share with his or her players the vision of the kind of team he wants and then make sure that they adopt it as their own.

Without this vision, this image of what the team is or can be, your team will lack direction. Colleen liked to use a story about Helen Keller in explaining to the team how important vision is. When asked how much of a handicap it was being born without sight, Helen Keller replied, "It's a far greater handicap to be born with sight but lack vision." What Colleen meant was that you have to imagine success and believe it's possible in order to attain it, and that the clarity of this image is what drives and motivates coaches and players.

On the road to rebuilding, after our defeat at the 1995 World Cup Championship, one of the first things we had to do was create a new image of the kind of team we wanted to be. In the past we had thought of ourselves as a blood-and-guts, blue-collar athletic team, but we needed to be more surgical, more precision oriented and much better in terms of possession while still maintaining those other qualities. So that's what we worked on and that's what we perfected.

In fact, at the end of the Olympics someone told Julie Foudy that the team had become a better team in possession. Julie replied, "Well, God, we'd *better* be a better team in possession; we've worked on it every day since the World Cup."

I remember bringing in tapes of the Men's European Championship and World Cup Games, especially tapes of the Dutch team to emphasize their ability to possess the ball. I also screened tapes of games with the Brazilian team, who exhibited an attitude that seemed to say, "We must win every game, but winning is not enough, we must win with flair and style and elegance."

Once we knew the kind of team we wanted to be, we had to set our goals. That process began in September 1995; we were at the Olympic Training Center in Southern California, and the decathlon team, including Dan O'Brien and Dave Johnson, was training at the site at the same time. Part of their training program included bringing in several motivational speakers, many of them Gold Medalists such as Bruce Jenner, Rafer Johnson, Bob Mathias, and Milt Campbell. The administrator of the team, whom I knew from my undergraduate days at Springfield College, asked me if we'd like to attend one of these sessions.

The next afternoon we went over to the track building and listened to Milt Campbell, who won the Silver Medal in the 1952 Olympic decathlon and the Gold Medal in 1956. During his speech, Campbell began to talk about Dan O'Brien.

"One day," said Campbell, "I went up to Dan and I said, 'Dan, what do you want to be? What do you want to achieve? What do you want to end up as?' And Dan looked at me and said, 'I want to be a great athlete.' 'You want to be a great athlete?,' I said, 'Well, Dan, then you're all done.' And I walked away."

The next day, Milt was out at the track and Dan O'Brien walked all the way across the infield to speak to him. "Hey Milt," Dan said, "what did you mean when you said I'm all done?"

"Well, Dan, you want to be a great athlete, right?"

"That's right."

"Well, guess what, Dan, you already are a great athlete. There's nothing more for you to achieve, and that's why I said, 'you're done.' What do you really want Dan? What do you really want to achieve?"

Dan thought for a moment and said, "Well, I want to be an Olympic Gold Medalist. I want to be the greatest decathlete in history."

Listening to Milt's story a light bulb went off and I said to myself, "My God, we have not—I have not—created a complete vision for my team." As we prepared our team that previous summer we never mentioned what we wanted to do, which was to win the World Cup Title and the Gold Medal. I had prepared the team to go to Sweden, confident and healthy, thinking that the outcome would take care of itself. It was a classic case of performance goals versus outcome goals.

And so, as a result of hearing Milt's story, from that day forward whenever we talked about the Olympics, I said, "Let's make no mistake about it, on August first, next summer, we want to be standing on the top podium, we want to have the feeling of the Gold Medal being put around our necks. That's our goal." And, for that matter, if I talked to the media or to anyone else, I would say, "Nothing will satisfy us until we're wearing the Gold Medal on August first."

So we constructed this new image of ourselves, knowing that we were no longer the best team in the world after the 1995 World Cup. We did it with videotape, we did it by talking about it, we did it with physical and mental training exercises. And slowly we formed a look that we wanted to project and a style that we wanted to play with. We began to nurture our own ideas about how we were going to achieve our goal and how we were going to win the Olympic Gold Medal. First we focused on becoming Olympic champions and then we envisioned ourselves as the greatest team this country had ever put together.

One day, as we were preparing for the Olympics, Colleen surprised the team with a box of navy-blue T-shirts that read THIS IS THE TEAM. NOW IS THE TIME. It was perfect for what we'd become because we weren't the same team we'd been. Now this was *the* team and everybody knew it. In fact, when one of the police officers who was part of our regular official escort would radio her colleagues from the bus, she would simply say, "I have *the* team here with me." It wasn't, "I have the U.S. team." It was, "I have *the* team." This anecdote reinforced the feeling that we were *the* team. We were a *special* team and this was the time for us to do something special.

From that moment on we started to zero in on that one goal, always keeping our eyes on *that* prize. The vision was clear. We knew what we wanted. If you asked any player at any time during the period between September 1995 until July 1999, before our first game, what our goal was, they would have told you it was to win the Gold Medal. Nothing else would be satisfactory.

Choosing Your Prize

One of the most illuminating and productive efforts you can make as a coach is to talk things over with your players. It's fun talking about goals and seeing players get passionate about them. It's also a good coaching tool because it creates energy and excitement that translate into your training regimen and the games.

At a meeting it's a good idea to create a dialogue. Ask your players things like

- What do we want to achieve?
- How do we want to achieve it?
- What do we value as people and as players?
- Do we want to be the thugs on the field, or do we want to be players who are above that?
- Are we going to be the kind of team that will win with skill and with sophistication?

Obviously, before you have this discussion with your players, you must have a fairly good idea of what you, as a coach, want for your team. For us it started out with discussions in the coaching staff. We'd ask ourselves, "What are we capable of this season? What are we after?" After we came to a consensus, the next question was, "How are we going to get there?"

After talking with your coaching staff, if you have one, you should hold the team meeting and ask your players the questions I mentioned earlier. Inevitably, as we did, you're going to have one of your leaders stand up and say, "We have to be fitter than anyone. We have to work harder than anyone else." That's a pretty strong statement for a player to make to her teammates. Stronger even than if it had come from one of the other coaches or from me because now it's coming from a peer. And then another might stand up and say, "We have to win every ball, so we have to have an intensity that communicates the attitude that 'It's my ball!'"

As a team we ultimately decided that we wanted to have that disciplined mentality that meant that if somebody whacked you, you didn't retaliate. On the Woman's National Team we used to think of it as "ice," which meant, "Nothing gets to us." If a referee made a bad call or an opposing player came up and bumped us unnecessarily, we just kept playing. We decided we couldn't afford to take yellow cards and end up having somebody important sitting on the bench because of yellow card accumulation when we competed in the medal rounds.

Setting Your Standards

Part of setting goals is setting team standards that you want to maintain. For us, part of that was respecting our opponents, which in effect meant respecting ourselves. We used to say, "The best thing we can do, when we play an inferior opponent, is to give them our best game, to hammer them if we can. We're not going to hold back. We're not going to beat them by just a little. We're going to try to play our best game, rather than simply slide through."

I know that might sound harsh to some people, but it's not: If you don't play your best against an opponent, it shows a lack of respect. I think that one of the accomplishments I'm most proud of from my tenure as coach is that we never lost to an inferior team, which meant we never lost because we were complacent. Of course we had games that weren't well-played games. And we lost games because we just didn't make the right play at the right time. But we never went in to play a lesser opponent at a lesser level and were beaten because of it.

Playing up to your standard is part of having your eyes on the prize. Every game you play ought to raise your standard of excellence. In our case, if we couldn't dominate in our region, how could we possibly dominate globally? To dominate and to win became part of our culture. It was the prize we kept our eyes on. It became a matter of practicing and competing and playing up to our expectations: not to be the best in just one event, but to be the best in *every* Olympic, World Cup, or international tournament.

I've often said that I believe I was a better person when I was part of that team. I had a more focused approach to where I wanted to go and how I wanted to get there. I was more tolerant of people, either on or off the team. And I was more considerate. I think we set higher standards of behavior for ourselves on the field, off the field and in life. We set the standard and then the team and each individual on it had to live by it.

When I think of "eyes on the prize," I think of players like Michelle Akers during our 1996 Olympic run. When we were trailing our arch rival Norway in the semifinals of the Olympics with fifteen minutes to go, we earned a penalty kick. There weren't a lot of players who wanted to take that penalty with the heavy burden of our Olympic success lying in the balance, but one player looked back at me and with every ounce of her body language said, "I want this kick." That was Michelle Akers.

I also remember a game we played in Trinidad and Tobago in 1994. Kristine Lilly was playing against a Canadian outside midfielder who was an exceptional player. They were going up and down the field and Kristine literally ran this excellent player into the ground. Her consistency was incredible; she never took a break. She never said, "Well, this time I won't run." Late in the game we won the ball, and Kristine took off again as she had all game long. Then, right in front of our bench, the Canadian player threw up her hands and said, "Go ahead, go ahead. Pass her the ball. I'm sick of chasing her." Kristine had taken this excellent player to a level where she literally gave up. This was an example of Kristine living up to her own standard of excellence and to the high standards of the team.

Setting Realistic Standards

If you're coaching a team at a lower level, you have to adjust your standards accordingly. In fact, setting standards too high can result in frustration for your players and for you. Be realistic. If your vision of the team is one of speed and agility and your players simply don't fit that vision, you'll have to adjust it. You must always take into account the ability of your players before you arbitrarily set goals for them. You can certainly raise the bar to a high level, but don't make it so high that it's impossible for your team to reach it.

Keeping the Vision Focused

Every team, no matter how good it is, is likely to lose its way once in a while, but the mark of a good team is how quickly it returns to the right path. If the focus of your vision starts to blur a little, there are some techniques you can use to get your team back on track. One method is to show your players how the vision manifests itself by using game footage if it's available. "This is what we look like, when we're 'on song,'" as the saying goes. "And this is what we look like when we've lost our way a bit." Then you can ask, "Which way would you rather play?"

If you've set a good foundation, if your team is talented enough and if you've set your standards high enough, the team itself will answer correctly without you getting in their faces and hammering away at them. All you have to do is ask, "What do you think?" Chances are the players will probably use harsher words about themselves than you as a coach ever would. To motivate and challenge players this way is not just nonthreatening, it's also more effective and empowering to your players than letting them know in no uncertain terms that they're playing terribly.

The key is for each player to know her role. Once she does, she won't have to worry about doing things that she's not good at and can concentrate on maximizing her strengths. All she has to do is execute her strengths consistently well. The equation is simple: *If I perform my role well and so do the rest of my teammates, then as a team we'll inevitably be playing great soccer.* In soccer we try to focus on putting the "best eleven" players on the team (with the focus on the collective synergy and on the entire team) rather than the "eleven best" players (with the focus on the individual talent of each player).

In order for this strategy to work, all players have to be completely tied into what their roles are. It's the coach's job to assign roles and keep things as simple as possible. There's a lot of truth to the old expression, "Soccer is a simple game played by complicated people." The game often becomes very complicated, of course, but it doesn't have to be. Once you show your players what their roles are and have made sure that each role is connected to individual talent, your vision can be built into a seamless, working mechanism. When each member of the team can buy into the prize, then you're on the road to success.

Consistency of Vision

One of the biggest mistakes coaches and parents make is that they raise the bar too high, or have unrealistic goals. As a coach, you must not only be consistent in what your vision is, but you must also be realistic. This is a dangerous word because sometimes I think "realistic" means underachievement. You still have to dream big. Obviously, I'm not saying everybody should go in saying, "We're going to win the championship; that's our goal." But I don't know if saying, "I'll be happy if we get to the second round" is enough of a goal. I'm still amazed when I hear coaches say that. It might be realistic, but it's not enough vision. If you're in this competition, you've got to think bigger than that.

Make sure you err on the big side rather than the little side because you'll never achieve greatness if you aim small. Remember the 1980 U.S. Olympic Men's Hockey Team? One of the techniques Coach Herb Brooks used was to consistently make fun of the Russians. Of the Russian captain he said, "That guy looks like Stan Laurel." Basically, what he was doing was taking the aura of invincibility that surrounded the Russian hockey team and poking holes in it for *his* players, who were a lot younger and a lot more impressionable. At the same time, he set very high goals for his team. They were going to beat the best teams in the world and win the Olympic Gold Medal, a task that everyone else thought impossible to accomplish. Very few people anywhere would have set the goals Herb Brooks set, and yet his team was able to achieve those objectives. And I strongly believe that if he hadn't set those high goals, while at the same time never letting his team take their eyes off that prize, they never would have won their Gold Medal.

Imitate, Replicate, Initiate

Keeping your eyes on the prize doesn't refer only to particular goals. Another aspect has to do with choosing a role model, someone to imitate in order to improve performance. Before the competitive part of the season even begins, it's a good idea to point this out to your team. Early in the season it's probably not possible to use members of your own team as role models except, of course, in the way they approach practice sessions, but you can certainly talk about more visible professional or collegiate players.

On our team we looked up to Joy Fawcett and Kristine Lilly for their unbelievable consistency. Or we pointed to Michelle Akers for her tenacity, or to Carla Overbeck and Julie Foudy for their leadership qualities. What we were doing was celebrating key parts of the equation that made these players and ultimately our team successful. At the same time, what we were really doing was identifying them as role models for other team members to imitate.

Joy Fawcett is an example of a wonderful role model. She is not only a gifted athlete but also a mother who, in 1999 as we were competing for the World Cup, had two lovely daughters (she now has three), and the team referred to her as Super Mom. Joy may never have been looked upon by the American media or the general public as one of the best players on the National Team, but she was. She wasn't a hard-knocks defender, a blunt instrument who would go out there and knock players over and take the ball away. Instead, she had intelligence, grace and skill that allowed her to pick an opponent's pocket, so to speak. If an attacking player was moving toward the goal, dribbling the ball, there wasn't any collision and there wasn't any foul. But there was a skillful and tenacious Joy Fawcett spiriting the ball away from her opponent and taking it up the field to begin the American attack.

Joy had an amazing consistency in the way she played, game in and game out. In 1996, when we were tied 1–1 with China in the Olympic Gold Medal game, it was Joy who broke in behind the defense, attracted the last defender, kept the attention of the goalkeeper and slid the ball across the goal to Tiffeny Milbrett, who scored the winning goal. In 1999, when we were behind against Germany in a very tense quarterfinal game of the World Cup in Washington D.C., Joy headed in a corner kick that gave us the lead, 3–2, and proved to be the winning goal.

The fact that Joy could play her position as flawlessly as she did and step in and play other positions, as well as come forward and score when we needed a critical goal, made her a perfect role model. With Joy it was all about consistency, and we celebrated that quality. That acknowledgment created a model for other players to imitate and try to replicate in their own unique way. In other words, we didn't want carbon copies of Joy Fawcett, we wanted each player to look to Joy, to see how she played to her potential and then do the same by playing up to theirs.

Choosing Your Role Model

As a coach or a parent, it's your job to help players choose the right role model. You can't always assume that your players are going to know who is the best person to imitate. Sometimes they're going to imitate a negative role model, someone who has bad training habits, is out of shape or plays inconsistently, often giving far less than maximum effort. You can't fabricate a role model, nor can you suggest somebody who only did something once or twice as the role model. It has to be someone who performs well on a continual and reoccurring basis. It's up to coaches and parents to identify these positive models and set a path that makes it easier for players to imitate them.

Here are some things you can do to help your players identify their idols. For instance, you can say, "Okay, I want you to evaluate your game, evaluate your performance. Tell me your strengths. Now give me three things that you know you could improve. Next, pick a teammate or an opponent or another athlete who is the image of how you want to perform. Tell me the three things that you really identify with in this athlete." The answer might be something like, "No matter what happens on the field, she never changes her facial expression. It's like nothing matters. If she makes a great play, if she makes a mistake, or if she has a bad call against her, there's no expression. This person is just the way I want to be on the field because I'm so emotional; I'm so up and down." Whatever it is the player wants to improve, she'll identify it with the help of your questions. And by asking those questions, you're helping her choose where she wants to go.

You can also do this exercise in reverse by saying, "Give me an example of who you don't want to be like. What are the things you really dislike about a soccer player?" The answer might be, "Well, she doesn't run all the time" or "She doesn't really look to pass the ball." After a while she'll give you four or five qualities and often, if you know the player, you'll see that many of the qualities she's mentioning are characteristics she demonstrates herself. We call this identifying "disowned material." This exercise helps players identify some of the aspects of their game that they don't like, which is helpful because it gives them the opportunity to make positive changes in their own behavior.

Besides using these exercises, you should also make it a practice to point out positive attributes of your players and celebrate them. This is what I call positive coaching. Most coaches stop practice when they see something negative, but I want to challenge you to stop play when someone does something positive. If you're taping games or practice sessions, stop the tape occasionally when you play it back later. Replay it and acknowledge the good play. What you will do is create images that other players, especially your younger players, are going to try to imitate. In essence, you are positively imprinting desirable actions, behaviors and performance.

On any team you're going to have some players who are great leaders naturally, who are vocal and take charge of the situation. Obviously these girls are going to be potential role models. This is something else you can take advantage of as a coach: Nurture this kind of leadership and praise these girls so that the other girls on the team will want to emulate them. Replicating this kind of behavior will give you the bonus of providing layers of leadership within the team, which is important to promote and sustain your team culture.

Here are a couple of examples of what I mean by layers of leadership:

In Brazil, in January of 1998, we had just come off an all-night flight. Danielle Fotopoulos was rooming with Julie Foudy. Danny was dead tired and all she wanted to do was go up to her room and collapse into bed. But as soon as they got up to the room Julie said, "I'm going downstairs to help unload the bus." No one asked her to do this, it wasn't her responsibility, and she wasn't asking Danny to go along with her. But Danielle saw what Julie was going to do and despite the fact that she was dead on her feet, she dragged herself downstairs to help unload the bus.

Then, a couple of days later, we were doing some pretournament fitness training on the field. It was very hot and I was working them hard. Our standard required the players to cross the line, not just reach it, before time expired. The last fitness exercise was very demanding and some players did not reach the standard. Mia hit the line just as I blew the whistle, meaning that she hadn't actually crossed it before time expired. Technically this meant that she hadn't made the standard. I was the only one who saw that she hadn't crossed the line in time, and I didn't say anything because of the heat and the overall horrible conditions. The players left the field and so did Mia. But she wasn't satisfied because of her own personal standard for excellence and so she actually came back onto the field and said to me, "Tony, will you time me again? I want to do it right." I did time her and this time she made the fitness standard.

You see, it wasn't acceptable to Mia that she hadn't actually completed the training exercise properly, even though she might have been the only one who knew it. So, she reran it, in the heat, in front of all her teammates, which included many of the young players on the team, just so she could make the standard. And it wasn't Julie's responsibility to unload the team bus, but she recognized that being on the team means acting in its best interests both on and off the field. To me these were wonderful examples for the team, representing behaviors that they could and did emulate.

Obviously, role models don't have to come from your own team. They can even come from a totally different discipline, such as the entertainment or business world, or from another sport entirely. You can also choose a team to be your role model, whether it's a team like the Women's National Team or the New York Yankees, the Los Angeles Lakers or the New York Liberty. The idea is to take the most positive attributes from the best teams and adopt them as your own.

Whoever your role models are, they should be realistic. Tiffeny Milbrett is another excellent example of a role model worth emulating. When Tiffeny gets the ball, she may not really have to make any moves because when an opponent comes to challenge her, she pushes the ball past her and she is able to run by the defender. She has these gears that no one else has, so I can't take any other player and say, "Okay, you see what Tiffeny just did? Do that." If the player has tremendous speed, then maybe she could emulate Tiffeny's performances. Most players, however, don't have the speed or quickness that Tiffeny has. Many players could get behind the defense, but they'd probably have to throw some moves and fakes in; whereas Tiffeny, with minimal fakes, just gets the defenders wrong footed, pushes the ball away and blows right by them. So if I have a player who has no speed and I ask her to imitate Tiffeny's moves, I'm setting her up for frustration and failure. You have to put people into situations where they can actually be successful at what they're imitating.

I would never challenge a youngster by saying, "Okay, imitate Michael Jordan or Marion Jones or Tiger Woods." Most athletes can't do what these superstars can do, but there are qualities of Michael Jordan and Marion Jones and Tiger Woods that you would want a player to imitate. With Tiger it might be his demeanor, his body language or his confidence as he plays. Watching Tiger, you learn how to walk the walk. If you walk around looking afraid, like a scared little rabbit, you'll probably play with the energy of that scared little rabbit. On the other hand, if you stride around with a little bit of a swagger, you carry and project a confident energy, then your play on the field is more likely to reflect that confidence and optimism.

Role models don't have to be drawn from among the most gifted players either. You might want one of your athletes to emulate players who are quiet but steady, who know their roles and perform them well. Tisha Venturini, who started in the Olympics in 1996, but was a reserve on the World Cup team in 1999, was my role model for those players who weren't starters but who came into the game from the bench. I wanted our players to imitate her. Tisha played a very important role because if you're a star or have been a star, you think you ought to be out there playing all the time and, generally, you're not very happy sitting on the bench. Well, here was a star who was a starter in the Olympics, had a Gold Medal, had scored our first goal in our first game in the Olympics, had scored our first goal in the second game of the Olympics, and yet she was now able to serve in this very different role and be a very positive role model to her teammates. By pointing out how Tisha accepted her new role and how she performed admirably in it, we were able to create a positive example for the rest of those who might start the game on the bench.

If you're coaching young children or are a parent of a child who's playing soccer, you're going to have to deal with kids who aren't starters. Using someone like Tisha as a role model goes a long way toward encouraging these kids to feel good about themselves and about their roles on the team.

Replicating Your Role Model

Sometimes players choose their own role models and without prodding try to replicate their play. But if they don't, it's up to the coach to help them. Here's an example: When I first joined the team as coach, I approached Mia Hamm and said, "Mia, for you to get to the next level, I just want you to develop consistency in your play." The reason I said this is that I had noticed that often when Mia didn't make a good play, she became very frustrated and upset with herself. The result was that for perhaps the next two to five minutes of play, I could see the frustration she was feeling, and I think it affected her play.

When we had our individual meeting, I pointed out to Mia that Kristine Lilly and Joy Fawcett were role models she could replicate. Using Kristine was especially helpful because Mia had tremendous respect for her and the level at which she performed consistently. So she began to look up to Kristine as a role model and tried to replicate the part of Kristine's game that she admired.

Here's a list for helping your players replicate the behaviors of their role models:

- Pick a specific behavior for the player to replicate. If you believe the player doesn't hustle enough, for example, suggest that she watch how her role model practices and plays enthusiastically.
- Suggest other role models to replicate if she's having trouble on her own. Not all role models exhibit every positive behavior, so you might have to guide your player by pointing out several different role models to emulate.
- The best way to teach athletes how to replicate their role models is to have them ask themselves, "What would so and so do in this situation?" Eventually they'll have a flash of insight about the way they want to be. Once they have an image of what they want to achieve, they can run with it awhile.
- I can't stress how important positive feedback is. The other day at a high school soccer game, I was sitting with another parent whose son had just entered the game. I could see almost immediately that this father was upset with what his son was doing on the field, and I could sense a problem. Fortunately, because I'd coached the son, I was able to share some positive statements before the father could deliver his negative comments. "Keep playing," I said. "That's good stuff. Keep trying it." Eventually I could feel that the boy knew he wasn't doing anything wrong and he kept working and working, finally scoring a goal.

As coaches and as parents, we have to create opportunities for our players. Part of it is teaching them to imitate and then to replicate what they admire. Another part of it is creating a safe environment where the girls can try new skills, behaviors and techniques without fear of failure or micromanaging parents and coaches who cause "paralysis by analysis" in athletes.

Initiating

It's natural for players to imitate qualities they admire and, eventually, they're going to add their own contributions to the mix. Imagine that you are asked to look at a picture of a country scene and then draw it yourself. In the beginning you'll just try to copy that picture as closely as you possibly can. After a while, however, you're going to start to embellish and improvise, drawing it in your own distinct way. That's exactly what's going to happen with your players.

In fact, it happened to me when I first became the head coach of the National Team. At first, I tried to imitate Anson Dorrance, the previous coach, because he was such a tremendous motivator. And then I tried to replicate the way he coached. But there was no way that I could be Anson. I had to pick and choose the best parts of his coaching style and bring those qualities into my own coaching. I had to have my own style. There is an inherent trap hidden here: If you try to copy someone else's style, or if you try to imitate others in ways that are inconsistent or unlike yourself, you will not be successful. You have to be able to imitate then replicate, and finally, initiate at your own authentic and genuine style.

An excellent example of a player bringing her own unique style and flair to the game is Brandi Chastain. When she first joined the team, I played her at left back, because I knew she would have no problem taking the ball and flighting it all the way across the field to the right back position. Now, of course, at the younger levels of soccer you never play a ball across your defense, but Brandi had the ability to flight the ball across the field and put it right on her teammate's foot. I wanted other players to learn this skill from Brandi. So through acknowledging its benefits and celebrating that ability when Brandi or any player performed it, I encouraged it as a skill for players to develop. Eventually the right back tried it and she replicated Brandi's pass. From that point on, other players had their own ways of initiating that pass. Brandi had showed them the impact of doing it successfully and they started imitating it in their own way. That's the way it has to be: Players are not always going to get from Point A to Point B in the exact same way, but if you allow them room to improvise and then guide them, they will get there more often and achieve even greater success than you might have expected from them.

COLLEEN'S TEAM-BUILDING EXERCISES

Here are two exercises that will help your team keep their eyes on the prize, create a vision for success and help develop the ability to imitate, replicate and initiate.

Piranha Waters

Equipment
Four cones to mark boundaries. Twenty to forty objects of various sizes, that is, athletic bags, balls, socks, or other articles of clothing. Stopwatch.

Space
An area of 10 by 10 yards, to 15 by 15 yards, depending upon the size of the athletes (the smaller the athlete, the smaller the area needed).

Number of Players
Two teams of any number of players.

Objective
To get your team, one blindfolded member at a time, from one side of the square to the other without being "eaten" by a piranha. The square area represents water. Only one blindfolded person is allowed in the water at any one time. You may designate one sighted captain or you can spread the wealth by alternating captains so that everyone has to lead at least once. The captain is the only one who can communicate while he or she tries to guide the blindfolded players, one by one, through the water without their being touched by any of the piranhas (the objects placed all around the square). If the player does touch one of the piranhas, there is a ten-second penalty. The team that gets all their members across the water fastest is the winner. A coach should be assigned to each team and add any penalty seconds resulting from touching a piranha.

Lesson
Players learn to keep their eyes on the prize while attempting to transfer the entire group safely to the other side. Sometimes we're "blind" and lose sight of our goals and sometimes things are clear. When there is clarity, it's easy to reach the prize. Sometimes there are obstacles and setbacks, but that's part of what the season is all about: navigating and negotiating through these challenges and setbacks and getting safely and successfully to the other side.

Debriefing
What was the hardest part of this exercise?
How did it feel to be completely responsible for the success of your teammates?
Who had the toughest job? Why?
What did you notice about yourself and experience when you were blindfolded?
How did your partner's communication help or hurt your success?
Were you able to "see" the finish line in your mind, even though you were blindfolded?
How can we apply these lessons to our session?

Bottoms-Up

Objective
To put yourself fully into the game.

In this progressive exercise, in order to improve and ultimately win, you must imitate successful people, then try to reproduce that success. But the ultimate progression is for the player to initiate, to create a new strategy for success, to stamp her own personality on the game.

Equipment
None.

Space
An open flat space, 10 yards by 10 yards for each team.

Number of Players
Two even teams of up to twelve players on each team.

The Game
Two people from each team sit face-to-face with their knees bent, in the position they would be in if they were finishing a sit-up. They are connected by holding each other's wrists. The goal is to lean back and pull at each other with equal force, without ever dropping the grip, in order to raise their bottoms so that they are both off the ground at the exact same time. Their feet must remain flat on the ground at all times. All the players on each team must accomplish this initial task in pairs and only when they do will the team move on to the next level. Cooperation and competition are the key words in this exercise.

Bottoms-up moves on to higher levels. For three people, all connected by their wrists and sitting in the same position as before (knees bent and feet flat on the ground), the goal is still to raise bottoms up at the same time. At this point, however, players will have to adjust because what worked before doesn't necessarily work now. When all three bottoms are raised, the team moves on to the next level—raising four players' bottoms off the ground at the same time—and it keeps going until all twelve people are connected and able to lift their bottoms up off the ground at the exact same time and without breaking the grip.

Along the way, teams will have to deal with failure and problem-solving skills. Failure should eventually foster success as the teams figure out which strategies work in each progressive challenge. The coach has to explain how this exercise relates to a game situation. For instance, the tactics we used against Canada may not work against China, that is, speed won't necessarily lead to victory in every game. Often different tactics might have to be used to achieve success.

Debriefing
How easy was the challenge at the beginning? Was there a change as competition progressed?

What does this exercise teach us?

Were the strategies you used initially the same ones you used throughout the challenge?

How did you and your teammates respond when you experienced setbacks and difficulties?

Did you and your teammates watch the other groups attempting the challenge? If so, what did you learn and how did it help?

How could you do better next time?

How does the exercise relate to the game of soccer?

TONY'S CHALK TALK

Dribbling Games

There are countless ways to teach players to dribble. My least favorite is to simply position cones and have players dribble around them. Is there ever a time for cone dribbling? Sure. When you want to play a relay game or something that has to be structured the same for everyone. But when you do that, just make sure it's a lot of fun . . . it's a game and not a drill!

Developing a player's ability to dribble can be achieved either by guided free-discovery dribbling or in a game designed to facilitate dribbling.

Dribbling Exercise

Option 1

Have all your players, all with their own balls, dribble in a confined area (you determine the size, but make sure you allow enough room to experiment, change direction and accelerate). Now give them the following commands (you can also think up others) while the players are dribbling:

- Dribble with the inside of the foot; outside of the foot; alternate using the inside and outside of your foot on every touch.
- Dribble in a circle clockwise; counterclockwise.
- Dribble in a circle using the outside of the foot only; the inside of the foot only.
- Dribble and on a command stop the ball dead; on the command, spin, turn and dribble in the opposite direction.
- Dribble around, don't touch anyone else's ball, don't bump into anyone, keep your head up and keep looking for open space.

- When the command is given, don't touch anyone else's ball, don't bump into anyone, keep your head up and keep looking for an open space, but dribble faster. Now faster, now faster! *Stop!* Repeat.

Option 2

- Use one ball for two players. The first player jogs while continually changing direction. The second player dribbles the ball and follows the leader as closely as possible. Players change roles on command.
- Create two teams by splitting up the partners. Using cones, create four or five random goals across the field. Teams score if one of its players dribbles the ball through an open goal. Periodically, the coach should stop the action to make tactical adjustments (i.e., "instead of attacking this goal where all the defenders are, pass the ball to a teammate who can dribble through a different goal").
- Remove all the random goals and use only the ends of the grid. If the grid is a rectangle, then sides A and B are goals that the red team defends and sides C and D are goals that the yellow team defends. The object is to dribble the ball over the other team's goal.

Coaching Challenge

Keep the activities fun and competitive. Don't coach only during the drills; these kinds of techniques can also be used during your scrimmages. Remember, soccer is a free-flowing game, so don't be afraid to coach during the game, not simply during drills. You can accomplish this by creating rules and restrictions to enhance one particular technique development. For instance, you can have your players dribble the ball across the line instead of passing or shooting it. This way, you've created an environment that will develop dribbling techniques for your players.

Questions and Comments

How long should an exercise last?

Dribbling exercises or others that are developing technique don't have to last long. Play them for 7 to 10 minutes and then change to another game. This allows your training sessions to change, letting you imprint the skills through the games.

CHAPTER 7

Catch Them Being Good

Don't whine. Find the positive in difficult situations.

—Tony DiCicco

Coaching doesn't stop just because the competitive portion of the season has begun. In fact, coaching is a season-long odyssey because it isn't possible to prepare your team for every contingency that will arise once competition has started. But coaching doesn't mean finding constant fault. Simply pointing out errors isn't coaching. As Benjamin Franklin once wrote, "Any fool can criticize, any fool can condemn, any fool can complain—and most fools do."

When you constantly find fault, you haven't constructively painted a picture of what to do, how to get it right. All you've done is create an atmosphere where people are living in a constant state of fear, apprehension and worry. There is a right way and a wrong way to correct your players' mistakes. I should know: I had to learn the right way.

In January of 1998 we were playing a tournament in China that included three of our great rivals: Norway, China and Sweden. We not only won, but we also didn't give up a goal against any of these elite teams. In that tournament, which was in preparation for the 1999 World Cup, each of our rivals had a number of young players and, naturally, these teams were experimenting a little with lineups and styles of play. But I didn't have inexperienced players and I didn't need to experiment. The outcome may have been successful, but I felt our performance was not up to the standards that we were capable of achieving. Frankly, I thought we played like crap, and in my frustration I crossed a line in being too critical. It's easy to do, especially if you've got an ideal vision of the way you want your team to play and they are playing below that standard. Frustration levels inevitably build.

After the tournament, my cocaptains, Carla Overbeck and Julie Foudy, asked to have a meeting with me. What they said shocked me.

"Are you going to cut us?" they asked.

"No, I'm not going to cut you," I responded incredulously.

"You're not going to cut us and bring in a lot of young players as these other teams are doing?"

"No, I'm not going to cut you," I repeated. "In fact, this is the team that's going to win the World Cup next summer. There may be a few other players that are going to challenge for positions on it, but this is the team."

"So," Carla said, "if you're not going to cut us, and we're the team, then why are you yelling at us so much?"

A good question. And one that made me stop and think about my behavior and my relationship to the team. First of all, by their coming in to see me to voice their fears and concerns, I knew that our relationship was a good one, that they trusted me. Second, I knew that they were probably right. I had overreacted and been too hard on them. Third, I knew that I had to correct the situation.

We left China and had a couple of weeks off before we were due to come together at the Olympic Training Center in Chula Vista, California. During that time I conferred with Colleen about my problem and she shared with me the phrase, "Catch them being good," which was really nothing more than emphasizing the positive rather than the negative.

When I arrived at training camp, I pulled my coaches together and said, "Okay, here's how we're going to approach this week. We're not going to coach the way we're used to doing. It's not going to be easy, but we are not going to correct everything we see that's wrong," which is the classic coaching style. Typically, coaches see something that's a mistake and stop the practice to point it out.

It's called a coachable moment. "Instead of coaching the way we usually do," I continued, "every time we see something that's wrong, we're going to store it for later; but when we see it done right, that's when we're going to coach it or celebrate it."

And that's exactly what we did. For example, if we saw Tiffeny Milbrett do something well, we'd say, "Everybody stop. Did everybody see Tiffeny's run here? Did you notice that bent run and how it tore the defense apart and opened up this big seam? That's why we were able to get that pass through there. This is what we're going to need to beat our great opponents. That was awesome. Great run, Tiffeny. Thanks for that demonstration. Let's play."

The difference between model A and model B was pretty drastic. At the end of the week the same two players, Carla and Julie, came up to me and said, "Tony, this was an awesome week."

I don't know if they consciously understood the difference in coaching, but they knew something was different, something that was very positive. And by the way, their play *was* awesome that week and I attribute it in large part to the fact that they felt so good about their game.

We continued to catch them being good after that training camp in spite of the fact that during the World Cup series, in the week between the semifinal game against Brazil and the final game against China, we were not playing very good soccer, perhaps because of the pressure. During that time I was sitting with my coaches, editing video, and saying things like, "Oh my God! We've got to show the team this. This—this is awful. We can't play like this against China. Look at this! It's awful! Make sure you keep this clip to show the team." Then I remembered Colleen's advice to catch them being good.

A short time later we had a scheduled meeting with the team and I realized I could not show them these negative clips or express my disappointment—I had to show them positive reactions. So by the time they came into that meeting and we started showing them the film clips, I had replaced all the negative video with clips showing things that had worked, and I said things like "Check this out. This is awesome! This is what we need to do this weekend against China. We'll be world champions if we play like that. Look at this pass! Look at this defense!" By removing all the negative clips and keeping only the positives, we probably didn't have as many clips, but they had a bigger, more positive impact.

Dealing with the Negative

At some point, of course, you have to deal with the negatives. In fact, part of my coaching philosophy is that early in the season it's okay to tear your team down a little bit. People don't want or need to have things sugarcoated all the time. They want to know that they can count on their coach to tell them the truth. The worst thing you could ever say to Mia Hamm when she didn't play well was, "Great game, Mia." That was an insult to her. What you could do was pick out one aspect of her game that was great and say, "Mia, you were awesome receiving balls back to goal." That would allow her to say to herself, "Well, okay, I was probably good at that even if other aspects of my game weren't good enough."

One of the best techniques you can use when you're about to give negative feedback is this simple feedback guideline. Ask, "Can I give you some feedback?" If the player says, "No," then respect the response and her inability to handle feedback at that time and don't give any. But if the player says, "Okay," then that's the signal that she can be open to what you have to say, so go right ahead.

Sometimes you must address mistakes on the spot, and sometimes you don't have to because you know that your player is aware of what she did wrong. But if you must speak up, it's always best to take the player aside and talk to her privately. It's not a useful technique to be critical of a player in front of her teammates, and it's simply bad coaching to belittle or overly criticize a player in public or in private. You have to be very careful about what and how you criticize because the last thing you want is for your players to fear failure. If they do, they won't play to their potential, and they will focus only on avoiding failure. Don't get me wrong: Every coach or parent has to be critical at one time or another. You have to tell it like it is, but there is a way to do it that allows the player to hear you. The other way just puts up walls.

For instance, in 1991, when we won the World Cup in China, I was the goalkeeper coach. Right before halftime we gave up a bad goal and went into halftime tied 1–1. I can't say I consciously did this, but I never mentioned the mistake. I didn't go up to Mary Harvey, the goalkeeper, and say, "What happened on that goal? What were you thinking?" Instead, I simply said, "Okay, here's what you're going to need to do in the second half . . ."

About a year later she came up to me and said, "I never told you this, but at halftime, when you didn't mention the mistake I made and simply told me what I needed to do in the second half, well, that had an unbelievable impact on me. It gave me a lot of confidence and allowed me to focus on the second half."

The Sandwich Theory of Criticism

The sandwich theory of feedback starts off with praise (the bread), followed by three pieces of information: what was done, what should have been done and why it should have been done (the meat). Then it finishes with one more piece of encouragement or praise (more bread). I use what is called the 4:1 rule. You mix in the positive with the negative by starting with a positive point or two, then you address the negative (which may be your key message) and finish with a positive. The 4:1 ratio doesn't always seem high enough; sometimes it's got to be 10:1 because some players view criticism as a personal attack. The ideal is to find that comfortable combination of correcting and celebrating, correcting and congratulating. And believe me, once you do, you'll find that it's an enjoyable and productive way to coach. Once you start celebrating a good play, not only will you make the individual player feel confident, but you'll also find that a glow will surround every other player on the team. Other players will want to achieve that kind of positive attention and they'll be motivated to strive for it.

Criticism

Criticism is a learned technique. As a coach, you must recognize when you're doing it. And if you're using negative criticism more than positive, you must change the ratio. Remember, body language and tone of voice also count as criticism. If a player does something and you drop your head, cross your arms and turn away, the message you convey is: "I'm disappointed and frustrated. Why have I invested all this time in you?" As coach, you've got to be very conscious of everything you're doing, both verbally and nonverbally. If a mistake is made and the player looks over at you (and believe me, players know when they've made a mistake), just smile and say, "Keep playing, keep playing. We'll get it next time."

Players are different in terms of how they react to criticism, and everyone needs feedback. But not everyone needs it the same way. Let me give you an example: In my SoccerPlus Camps program, I had an excellent coach on my staff, but he was the kind of coach who pushed the kids and kept pushing them and rarely, if ever, said anything positive.

Eventually I approached him and said, "Listen, I know you're on their side, but they don't. You're pushing them and when they eventually do what you want, when they finally achieve it, you can't just assume each of them is saying, 'Oh, Coach pushed me hard and it's made me a better player, so thank you, Coach.' Because what they're really saying is, 'I'm glad I did it because I got this jerk off my back.' So what you need to do is walk up to the player and say, 'Hey, I pushed you hard and you responded, and I really respect the way you went after it.' If you do that, you'll create a bond between you and that player as well as reciprocal positive energy."

I've found that sometimes you're so in tune with your players, so much on their side, that when they make a mistake, you actually suffer along with them. But they don't see that. They only see the criticism. As a coach or a parent, you have to be conscious of this dynamic. Your communication will be in the form of body language. You will react to a missed play, and what you're feeling and what they are seeing may be at opposite ends of the spectrum.

All coaches and teachers are generally after the same outcome. We want higher levels of performance. Everybody's performance falls off from time to time and everybody makes mistakes, but the job of a coach is to maintain a positive, consistent vision, even if the players sometimes falter and lose focus.

Battling the Negative Spiral

I remember coaching middle school basketball when I was a teacher in Bellows Falls, a small town in Vermont. One day, the team had a game in Brattleboro, a larger town nearby. Having more kids to draw from, they were clearly a better team—bigger, stronger, faster and more skilled. Yet it turned out to be one of my most rewarding coaching experiences. We didn't win—I don't think the game was ever that close and we must have lost by almost twenty points—but the effort my players gave was awesome. We played at a level far beyond our normal capabilities. At the end of the game a teacher from Brattleboro came up to me and said, "You were so positive with your players. I really thought you did a great job."

I've thought about that game over the years and I've come to the conclusion that I was secure enough in myself that even while we were getting badly beaten, I wasn't taking it as a personal defeat. In fact, I was delighted with my team for playing the way they were playing, for the effort they were giving. So from the sidelines I was constantly congratulating them, and that only enhanced their play.

This is a coaching methodology I've always followed, in part because I've seen the opposite tactic and how it can be very destructive, turning into a negative spiral. Let me show you how a coach can impact this dynamic: Last winter I was watching my son play basketball, and the team was really pumped up because they were playing against a very good team. They played hard and it was a fairly even game. Clearly, however, the other team had more experience and they were slightly better, but my son's team was holding their own. Soon the coach started to pull players out and demonstrate both verbal and nonverbal displeasure in their performance. He'd look at his players and say, "What the heck is going on out there?" He'd stand up and he'd make a substitution, kind of a spur-of-the-moment thing, saying only, "Get in there for him." The boy would come out and the coach would just look at him. It was a negative process and the next time those players got back into the game, they weren't playing at the same intensity level at which they'd started.

The next time they were put into the game, they were again pulled out for all the wrong reasons. They were never given any positive feedback like, "You're playing hard. I like it. The ball's not dropping for you now, but keep shooting." It was always the negative, "You can't dribble into that double team" or "Why are you taking that shot?" As the game went along, you could see their performance literally spiraling downward. They had less intensity, they were less free to play, they were more afraid of making mistakes.

That's the kind of impact a coach can have. Coaches and parents have to realize that their words, their body language and the way they present feedback is going to have an impact on performance. Negativity is antivision. Instead of building toward a positive vision, it tears it down, yielding ineffective and inappropriate coaching or parenting.

A coach or parent has to be much more positive than corrective or negative. You've got to pat your players on the back. You've got to say, "Great play." Or "Hey girls, did you see that pass? It was fantastic. Let's see more of that." You've got to break the negative spiral that will eventually bring your entire team down. If you don't, you'll put them in a position from which they are less likely to win because they won't have the confidence to make the play when the game is on the line.

COLLEEN'S TEAM-BUILDING EXERCISES

Bean Bag Shuffle

Objective

To hone problem-solving techniques and foster cooperation among team members in order to achieve success through competition between groups to establish the best team. Perhaps, more important, it provides an opportunity to reveal an athlete's standard for competitive excellence as a member of her own team, as an opponent striving for victory, and as an individual competing against previous personal best performance.

Equipment

One stopwatch for each team, one small bean bag per team (you can buy them in a store or make your own).

Space

An open field or gym.

Number of Players

Divide your group into two or three teams of six to eight individuals.

The Game

Provide each team with one small bean bag and have the teams stand in a circle; it can be any size they choose. Set the challenge: The goal of this activity is to see how fast you can pass the bean bag from person to person so that everyone in the group has completely handled it and individually passed it on to another team member. Simply touching the bean bag does not count; it must be *completely* "handled and individually passed."

Assign a stopwatch coach (a trustworthy, competent timekeeper) to each group. On the signal "ready, set, go," teams begin to pass the bean bag around the circle as fast as they can while still following the rules. If the bean bag hits the ground, players must start again from the beginning.

Establish a winner based on time. Record that time and then ask, "Can you do it faster?" Let them try. Continue to record the times for each team. Then ask, "Can you do it faster still?"

Lesson

Eventually teams will learn to move very close together to make an even smaller circle that looks like just a mob of people. They will learn that they can hand and pass the beanbag much faster, more efficiently and in a single motion if they change their distance from one another and alter their team's configuration.

At first, players they think they're doing well, but as the game progresses you'll be raising the bar and putting more responsibility on the players, telling them in essence: You did well, but now can you do better?

Debriefing

What did you learn from this exercise?

What helped you be more successful?

Did you feel excited and motivated to lower your time, or did you already feel you were fast enough?

Was there any difference in your experience when the goal was to beat the other team instead of beating your previous best time?

What would you do differently next time?

How does this exercise relate to a game situation?

TONY'S CHALK TALK

Heading for Beginners

Heading is a skill unique to the sport of soccer. There have been studies to prove and disprove that heading is dangerous, yet heading is an integral part of the game, so it's important to make sure we teach players how to head safely and effectively. For the youngest players, age ten and older, heading should be introduced slowly and practiced sporadically with the emphasis on showing them how to head safely with proper technique, which means proper contact with the forehead and the ball.

Option 1

For an introductory game of heading, bring out slightly deflated soccer balls or even nerf balls. Assign each player a partner. Partner 1 heads the ball from her own hands back into her own hands and scores 1. Then she passes the ball to partner 2, who catches the ball and heads the ball from her own hands back into her own hands and scores 2. Repeat this over a 30-second time limit and compare scores. Sometimes the movement of the ball from the hands really never happens. That's fine, so long as there is proper head contact (with the forehead and the ball).

The next progression is to have partner 1 serve a ball to partner 2, who heads it back to partner 1. The action is repeated. Each time there is a head and a catch that counts as goal. On the coach's signal, the partners switch roles. At the end, scores are compared and they play again.

Option 2

Play a game of handball in which there are two goals (usually just a line to be crossed) and two teams. The object is to pass the ball between hands and then score. The ball must be passed to a teammate who heads the ball across the goal line to score.

The next progression is to have two teams play, but this time the passing sequence goes from hand to head to hand and repeats. In other words, for a player to move the ball down the field, she has to toss it to a teammate who heads it back to her or to another teammate who can catch it and so on.

Questions and Comments

How long do I stay in a game like this?

I usually introduce these games during the later stages of warm-up, which means they will last 10 minutes or less. Early on, players won't have much success, so don't try to force them to learn faster than they can. As they get the hang of it, they will enjoy the keep-away format of the game and the heading becomes second nature.

What do I do for the player who just won't head?

Be patient. Work with her on your own for a few minutes before or after practice. Help her break down the mental block and stay in the most elementary stages of heading as long as necessary until she is ready to move to the next level.

Coaching Challenge

Because heading is unpopular with players and coaches, it is often avoided during training sessions. As coaches, we need to take on the responsibility of teaching proper technique so that players learn very early how to head safely. Be creative, be realistic, be responsible.

CHAPTER 8

Inner Winner, Outer Champion: Developing Self-esteem

The first step to winning is being comfortable with it. Feeling it. Embracing it. Being obsessed by it, but also enjoying it.

—Tony DiCicco

In order to be a winner, you must think like a winner. Unlike the Missouri license plate which proudly announces itself as from the Show-Me State, some things have to be believed before they can be achieved. You have to have faith and you have to have the belief in yourself before others will see it in you.

Now, especially as you embark upon the competitive part of the season, it's your job as a coach (or as a parent) to instill confidence in your players. You must help them believe they have the talent to win because people almost always behave in ways consistent with how they see themselves. And if your players see themselves as winners, that's how they will perform. Look at the New England Patriots' 2001 Super Bowl Championship run. No one thought them good enough except their coaches and themselves. Having that kind of confidence is an "inside job," and it has to start inside each person and within the team.

After our team won Olympic Gold in Atlanta in 1996, they proudly marched out onto the field and took their places on the top level of the podium for the presentation of their Gold Medals. Later, in the locker room, after the stadium had emptied out, a few of the players came up to me and said, "You know, Tony, it's the strangest thing, but when we were up there and those medals were put around our necks, it actually felt like we'd been there before."

This didn't surprise me because the truth was they *had* been there before, though only in their minds. And there was good reason for that: For almost a year Colleen and I had prepared the team for that very moment, the moment when they would experience being champions. In other words, they were inner winners well before they were outer champions.

Oddly enough, the person who first comes to mind in terms of being an inner winner is Carla Overbeck, our captain. Carla was the one who had guarded our team psyche by knocking on wood and never talking about the Gold Medal or winning the World Cup. She did this partly to keep a humble presence and not to put too much pressure on us and partly to protect team confidence because our collective morale had taken a blow the summer before when we were eliminated from the World Cup. Initially Carla was reluctant to make bold statements about our real vision, but more and more frequently I would hear her announce to the media something like, "We know how difficult our group is and we know that there are other great teams in the field, but our goal is the Gold Medal and I feel sorry for any team standing in our path." As I had hoped, Carla and the entire team embraced our vision and were able to articulate it. Very clearly and directly she would say to the team, behind closed doors, "This is our championship. No one's gonna bleepin' stop us. We're going to win the Gold Medal."

As the number-one leader of our team, Carla's embrace of the vision helped the team buy into our goal and recapture the confidence that we needed to win Gold. In the end, it wasn't so much about changing one person but rather about how one person changed us collectively, as a team.

When this transformation happens within a team, when the players embrace the same collective vision, it results in a sense of freedom. Let's face it and be honest—that was our goal—so why try to hide or deny it? That was what we wanted, so why not embrace it? Why not acknowledge it to ourselves and to the world? The reason many people shy away from this level of honesty or hide their ambitions is because they think that if they don't achieve everything they set out to do, they will be less embarrassed if they haven't admitted their real hopes and dreams. Well, the truth is it's just as embarrassing and it's just as painful whether we acknowledge our goals or not. So, let's go for it!

You're not always going to be able to reach your goal, but you will achieve more than you ever thought possible by creating a vision and nurturing your players' confidence so that they will go for it. As you move toward that positive vision, no one will ever be able to take that effort away from you or diminish what you have achieved. As the saying goes, It's not the destination, it's the journey.

Imagery Exercises

Being an inner winner starts with small steps. First, your players must believe in themselves, in their own abilities. For instance, when you're working on a particular athletic skill, or making one play or achieving one task in a given day, it will boost your players' confidence and make it easier to be successful if they can *feel* themselves being successful at it.

One way you can do this is by using imagery techniques. Imagery is an extremely powerful tool for training and manipulating performance. You don't want players to be afraid of failure because they won't try to win, they'll just try to avoid failure. Imagery is just as important for coaches as it is for athletes.

In the middle of the day, with the sun beaming down after a hard training session, I would have the players lie down on the grass, relax and do imagery training. I had them visualize performing their unique abilities on the soccer field over and over again. I would say, "Imagine in your mind what you do well. If you're a great header, visualize yourself winning headers. If you're a great defender, visualize yourself stripping the ball from an attacking player. If you're a great passer of the ball, visualize yourself playing balls in. If you've got great speed, visualize yourself running by players and receiving the ball." I made a special point of saying, "Visualize the special skills that separate you from the rest—the skills that make your team better because you possess them."

We engaged not only in team imagery sessions, but also in

individual imagery practices that Colleen facilitated. She would help players create and re-create every aspect of the game they were about to play. Players were encouraged to use all five of their senses as well as their emotions to refine and successfully execute their own best performance.

As a coach, obviously, you're bound to come across players who won't or can't buy into the value of imaging techniques or can't create their own successful images. There are players who will say, "There's no way we can win. There's no way I can do this." It's a common situation and a classic case of what I call a negative feedback loop. In this instance, rather than being the result of a nonsupportive or critical coach or parent, as discussed in the previous chapter, it is self-generated by the athlete. A player says to herself, "Here comes the ball and I'm going to kick it into the goal." She kicks at it and she gets a little piece of it, or she misses it, or she hits it over the goal. The next thing she says to herself is something like, "I always miss that shot. Why can't I ever make that shot? I suck." Something inside that player, often subconsciously, says, "Okay, when I see this situation, I know I don't make the shot. I know how I react. I know I get mad at myself." As a result, the player creates a negative feedback loop. In essence, it becomes a negative, self-fulfilling prophecy.

The first job of a coach (or the player herself) is to identify that kind of negative thinking because unless it's dealt with, the player will become an inner loser rather than an inner winner.

There are several techniques to break this negative loop. One method is called cue word or performance cues, which are designed to stop negative orientation and refocus on the positive. Over the years, I've heard different cue words, but whatever the cue word is, it must serve to break the destructive thinking pattern and get the player to think positively. For instance, you can have players use a word like "focus," at which point they stop thinking about their error and bring themselves back into the game. The idea is to prevent the player from looking back and to focus instead on one particular play at a time in the here and now.

Another technique is to encourage the player to replay the event in her mind, just like a video camera—rewinding the action to the moments before the play and instead of seeing the play as it was, see herself performing it exactly the way she wanted to. And if she needs to, she can rewind it again and do the same thing. Through this process the inner performer is trained to see how she wants to accomplish a particular play and at the same time the inner winner is trained to succeed.

Park It!

Another essential tool your players can use is a phrase Colleen introduced that says, "Park it" (a technique first introduced by Terry Orlick in his work with Canadian Olympic athletes). She would say to an athlete, "Leave it in the parking lot. We'll go back to it later. We know where it is because we've parked it in a space in our mind and then we've walked away from it. And we walked away in order to go about the most important task at hand: this play, this game, this moment. Right now, the best thing you can do with the error is to park it and get on with your task." What this does is allow the player to refocus, which is a very important technique in successful performance. Unfortunately, there are many coaches and parents out there whose method of approaching tasks is to show their players and children how much they *can't* accomplish rather than how much they *can* with positive thinking, organization, planning, vision and discipline.

If you are able to get some of your players, especially the leadership of your team, to think this way, then Park it will become an infectious phrase within the entire group. Eventually everybody starts emulating the technique and applying it to many situations. As a coach, if you encourage your leaders to stop, park the negative, refocus and play in the now (not the past or the future), you will begin moving your team in the right direction. Over the years, I've seen this positive dynamic at work and I've seen how both individual and team confidence is tied into it.

Part of the job of a coach or teacher is to show your players not only how good they are individually but how good they are collectively—how each player on the team fits so comfortably and easily together, making the entire group better. This isn't always easy, especially when you've got a team that's had a recent history of losing or a team that's only mediocre in ability.

Remember, nothing comes quickly. There are no quick fixes. You must take small steps. It's a mistake to think that you can go from being at the bottom of the barrel to being Olympic champions in one quick step. Success begins with having each player on the team learn the lesson of the inner winner/outer champion and then, with the coach's help, molding that sense of personal confidence into the entire team's vision that the group can achieve the ultimate goal. As relief pitcher Tug McGraw kept repeating to his Mets team of 1986, "You've got to believe that you can do it."

COLLEEN'S TEAM-BUILDING EXERCISES

The Trust Walk

Objective
To develop leadership and responsibility among athletes by requiring every team member to take turns as the sighted guide with complete control over the safety, challenges presented, and quality of the experience of her teammates. Conversely, since each athlete also takes a turn blindfolded, players learn to trust their teammates, to accept and follow instructions, to gain confidence in a task in which they feel emotionally vulnerable and physically challenged, all within an unpredictable environment.

Equipment
A blindfold

Space
Soccer field, woods, gym, anywhere you're having practice

Number of Players
Teams of two

The Game
One blindfolded partner, one sighted—the sighted person cannot touch the blindfolded person and is completely responsible for the care and safety of the blindfolded partner. Designate the time for each person to be blindfolded before switching, say 2 to 3 minutes for younger athletes and 5 minutes for older ones. Both people walk slowly together using only verbal means of communication. All verbal directional commands—to go over, under and around objects—are up to the sighted person. Participants are required to trust themselves and have confidence in their teammates. Self-esteem is best improved by successful experiences such as this one. Athletes initially tend to feel very vulnerable and insecure in a trust

walk, but as they grow more confident, they begin to take more risks and gain confidence from the experience.

Debriefing

What is the point of this exercise?

What was it like to be completely responsible for both the challenge provided and the safety of your teammate?

Did you have any difficulty or hesitancy trusting your teammate when you were blindfolded? Why? Why not?

Why is trust in your teammates important?

How did your sighted teammate's tone and demeanor change your experience when you were blindfolded?

How did it feel when you and your teammate successfully did something difficult together?

How does this actively relate to the game of soccer?

TONY'S CHALK TALK

Passing

Passing is not a skill that I separate from the game very often. I train passing by putting players in a possession game or a 4v4 short-sided game. However, there are times, often during warm-ups, when passing exercises are appropriate. The best passers of the ball can use the inside or outside of the foot and can also use the instep surface to pass over longer distances. The following are a couple of passing exercises for you to experiment with.

Option 1

Create groups of four or five players. Find a space that will allow for each pass to be between 5 to 10 yards. The object is to ping the ball from player to player in a one-touch sequence. This means that as the ball comes to a player, she has one touch to pass it to the next player. It's important that players are never standing during this exercise, so when a player passes she must follow her pass with a few quick sprinting strides, going to the opposite side from where she has passed the ball. There are no grid lines or cones. This is a free-flowing ball and player movement exercise that when done well shows excellent technique. Occasionally, players can use the first touch to control the ball and then the second touch to pass it, but they should try to do everything in one touch whenever possible.

You can make this a game by giving each group of four 30 or 45 seconds to complete as many passes as they can. Only count one-touch passes. When performed well, this exercise has an attractive sharpness to it.

Option 2 (more advanced)

This exercise, which the Women's National Team used during pregame warm-ups, is a passing sequence involving three players. Two of the three players are lined up vertically about 25 to 30 yards apart; the third player is lined up between the two others. Player 1 has the ball and, using the inside or outside of her foot, she is going to bend the ball around the central player. The central player moves to support player 2, who is receiving the ball. Player 2 one touches the ball to support player 3 and player 3 passes it back to player 2, who serves around player 3 to player 1. Player 2 and player 3 change positions and player 2 now sprints to support the receiver, player 1, and the exercise repeats itself. Allow the players to experiment with outside and inside bending balls. You will be surprised how quickly some athletes will pick it up.

Questions and Comments

How does a player bend a pass?

If a right-footed player hits the ball with her instep, the ball should travel true. There may be a slight right-to-left bend of the ball, but don't worry about that. If the same right-footed player hits the ball slightly off center with her instep toward the inside of the foot, there will be a counterclockwise spin on the ball that will bend it right to left. If the player hits the ball off center toward the outside of her foot, a clockwise spin will bend it left to right. Using the left foot puts the opposite spin on the ball.

The key is to hit the center of the ball, adding a follow-through to the outside or inside of the ball, which will achieve the desired spin and bend on the ball.

Coaching Challenge

This exercise is about teaching new and different techniques to your players. If you are not proficient enough to do it, make sure they are exposed to the best coaches so they can experience the game at the next level. You need to demand that your right side flank midfielder can bend the ball down the line so that it spins into the forward, who is running toward the corner, rather than spins out of bounds.

CHAPTER 9

Feedback Is the Breakfast of Champions: Communicating with Your Team

The first thing a manager or coach needs to learn is how to listen.

—Tony DiCicco

The season is under way and, whether your team is playing well or not, there are always areas where you, as a coach, know there's room for improvement. Perhaps certain players aren't playing up to their potential. Or perhaps the team just isn't gelling the way you'd like them to. It's your job as coach to point out those areas to individual players and to the team as a whole, but the question is, how do you do it?

Just as breakfast is the most important meal of the day because it sets the tone for the energy and stamina for the rest of the day, appropriate feedback is essential for peak performance. Communication is the art of making a difference.

I don't think I'm a particularly great communicator: It's something I have to work on constantly. The first thing you have to learn about communication is how to listen and observe. As a coach, you can never quite grasp the full impact of what you say and also what you don't say. There is, in effect, a gap between what you think you're communicating to your team and what they're actually receiving. As a coach, I have a tendency to think that I'm pretty much getting my ideas across and that my team knows where I'm coming from and what I expect from them. But I've learned over the years that's not always the case.

Here's an example: One day, Joy Fawcett came into my office and said, "Tony, can I talk to you?" Now, first of all, for Joy to say, "Can I talk to you?" was something of a surprise because Joy never talks. We had a lot of respect for each other, but we really didn't communicate very much, perhaps because we both subscribe to the old adage, Silence is golden.

I said, "Sure, Joy, sit down. What's up?"

"Are you going to cut me from the team?"

At that moment nothing could have been further from my mind, so I was taken completely aback, wondering where on earth she would get such an idea. Joy was the consummate professional and clearly one of the best players in the world. It was so ridiculous that I even remember thinking, *Don't break out laughing, Tony; she's serious.*

"Joy, I'm trying to clone you, to create more of you, not cut you."

What I realized afterward was that I had thought the kind of feedback I was giving, the body language and the speech, was saying, "Joy you're unbelievable." Obviously that wasn't the case. I think that's the most important lesson a coach needs to learn about feedback: What you think you're saying may not always coincide with what your players are hearing.

Here's another example to help illustrate the point. We had very talented players on the bench and one of them was Tisha Venturini. Tish was a former starter for us, but as we were making final preparations for the World Cup, I could sense she was a little lost. Her confidence was wavering and I hadn't been giving her what she needed in feedback. At the same time, we had Danielle Fotopoulos, the young star who'd not only broken but had also blown away Mia's and Tiffeny's collegiate scoring record. But at that time I wasn't getting what I needed from Danny either—another lack-of-feedback casualty. Three months before the World Cup we were going to play China in an exhibition game in Hershey, Pennsylvania, so in my individual meetings with both players I was able, finally, to give them meaningful feedback to help clarify their roles within the team and boost their play; it carried us right through to the World Cup.

With Tish I said, "You're a goal scorer; you've always been a goal scorer. And you know what, Tish, because of the respect you carry on this team and because your teammates know that you can score goals, they look for you when you're in the game. Your role, as I see it, is to be able to go into a game and score a goal whenever I put you there, either at the beginning, the midway point, or the end. That's your role on this team."

I said it succinctly. I said it clearly. I said it emphatically. Tish didn't have to read through the lines. She didn't have to intuit what I wanted from her. She knew exactly what her role was, what was expected of her, and she could now go out and do it, which she did—sooner even than I had thought realistic.

When Danielle came in for her meeting, I did the same thing. I said, "Danny, there is one thing I know you can do on the field, and that is put the ball in the back of the net. You need to put it in more consistently, you need to put it in with fewer chances. But the fact is, you've put the ball in the back of the net on every team you've ever played for. That's your role on this team. I hope you can do a lot of other stuff, but when you get into the game, that's your role—to help make or score goals."

That night we played China and we played a great game. In fact, it was the best game we'd ever played against China. We dominated them for ninety minutes, but the score was 1–1. In the eighty-fifth minute I put Tish and Danny in the game and when they went in, they both fully understood what their roles were. I could see it! And sure enough, Danny became our target. We were sending balls to her head, and the Chinese players were crawling all over her body trying to get to the ball, and they eventually fouled her. Someone quickly put the ball in play to Mia, who sprinted down into the corner. She looked up before serving the ball and who was there but Tish. Mia crossed the ball to Tish, who, after a scramble in front of the goal, smashed the ball into the net, and we wound up winning the game.

All this came from simple feedback. I told them what I perceived their best roles to be and how I saw them helping the team, and they went out onto the field looking for just those opportunities. I'd given them something they could hold on to, something that made sense to them. That's what feedback is all about—meaningful communication.

There's another side to feedback too. When you give it, you establish an understanding on which you must follow through. I believed in Tish. I knew she could get us a goal when we needed it. Other people argued that there were better players on the bench, but as far as I was concerned that was Tish's role, and she had bought into it. We had established a trust and an understanding. It was only logical for me to choose her as my substitute with only minutes remaining in that game against China. The fact that she scored the winning goal may have surprised many people but not Tish and not me.

Getting Your Point Across

Feedback and constructive criticism are important. While some people can give too much feedback, rambling on until players just shut down and hear nothing, my experience has been that players look for more rather than less of it. For instance, Michelle Akers, one of the best players in the world, often asked me, "What do I have to do to get better?" And then, being as goal directed as she was, she'd add something like, "Since you don't have a lot of time to talk, Tony, just give me what I need to do and let me get the hell out of here."

Feedback can blow up in a coach's face, however. I remember a conversation with a player who I thought was a very important part of our future, but just wasn't ready to make the Olympic team. I tried to tell her that by explaining what an awesome player she was and how she would be part of our legacy for many years to come. I told her she was the victim of a numbers game and for this tournament there were other players positioned ahead of her. I thought I was being constructive but, instead, the player just heard, "This is my dream, to play in the Olympics, and he's cutting me." She heard only the negative, that she wasn't going to make the team, and she couldn't grab on to or connect with the positive.

Before giving any feedback, it's best to take a moment to center yourself. If the feedback is going to be worthwhile, you have to be tactful. You have to know what your player needs to hear, why she has to hear it and how best to score a positive impact in the particular circumstances. Once again it's best to use the ratio approach to feedback: four positives for every negative. With some players, and you'll know who they are, the ratio will need to rise perhaps as high as ten to one. Always start and end with positives and insert the corrective feedback in the middle (the sandwich theory). For instance, let's say I have a player with incredible talent, but for some reason I can't get her to put it out there on the field. She's not letting herself play up to her potential because if she does and she's not successful, she has nowhere to fall back. Here's what I would say to her: "You have world-class dimensions. Your speed is outstanding. You have the ability to dribble and blow by potential defenders, which is a dimension that is very uncommon on the world stage. You can score in the attacking zone or defend in the defending zone, which is a tremendous asset to the team. But you need to play on your cutting edge. You need to stop fearing failure and let it all hang out. You need to dig deep and find out what you really want to invest as a player. Because you have dimensions that are world class, you can play and be a personality player as a striker or a dominant player as a defender. That's how good you can be."

Different Strokes for Different Folks

There are all kinds of coaching styles and you have to use what feels most comfortable. Some coaches are right out there on the edge— you always know exactly what they're feeling. They are blunt and direct. With these coaches, communication is not the problem so much as *how* they're communicating. Sometimes they rant and rave, either at their own players or at the officials. And one thing to be aware of is that often the personality of the coach is picked up by the team. If you start complaining about every call, accusing the referee of screwing your team, that attitude is going to become part of the team ethos.

I have to admit that there have been times when I've let my emotions get the best of me. I've had run-ins with officials and once, when I was thrown out of a game, my ten-year-old son Alex was sitting on the bench with the team. I can still remember the look on his face as the game administrator at Soldier Field in Chicago was taking me from the bench to the locker room. Even though I disagreed with the official, I realized I'd made a terrible mistake, so I apologized to the officials, to my team and also to Germany's coaches. And yet, in that case, something did happen that made me feel a little better. It was when Mia Hamm came up to me afterward and said, "Thanks for protecting me."

Other coaches display their passion and interest differently. They always seem to be in balance, unflappable and calm. Yankee manager Joe Torre is a perfect example. If you watch him in the dugout during a game, his face betrays little emotion and his arms are often folded benignly across his chest. I've never seen him openly berate a player. I've never seen him lose his cool. Sometimes with coaches like this, players may not know if they've made a mistake or have their great plays acknowledged. No matter what style you effect as a coach, the key is to understand both the advantages and disadvantages that your style has on players. Players and coaches alike will be more successful if they understand each other and communicate honestly and consistently. Certainly, you need passion, you need to have (and sometimes demonstrate) emotion, but you also need to keep things on an even keel.

The Coachable Moment

One of the questions a coach frequently has to grapple with is how and when to offer feedback. Often it comes in what is called the coachable moment. This occurs when you see something happening at the moment, either on the playing field or in a practice session, that you can comment on. It can be very powerful when you find that coachable moment and are able to give positive feedback. Usually this is something you want the whole team to hear.

Sometimes I have feedback for the whole team, while other times it's just for an individual. It's also possible that during feedback to an individual, the entire team will benefit from the message. Often when we are out on the field, I will stop the play and have the whole team celebrate a play or decision made by an individual player. This is a tremendous way to build individual confidence and self-esteem and at the same time spread accolades throughout the team to show them the way the coach wants a particular situation handled. "What a great pass, Kristine! That was awesome! You relieved pressure. Out of twenty-four players on the field, you found the exact person you needed to get the ball to, and you put it right on her foot. That was just a great play and I'm glad I was here to watch it!"

When you can give that kind of feedback, it's great for Kristine, and it's also great for her teammates. It builds up the whole team.

• Team Feedback

You can initiate feedback in as formal a setting as a group meeting in a classroom or you can simply gather the players together before a training session. Let's say you're concerned about the fitness of several members of your team. You can say something as simple and general as "I'm concerned with our fitness." With girls, who tend to internalize everything, every one of those players will think you're talking about her. If I said that the same thing to a boys' team, most of the guys would be thinking, "Coach is right. Some of these guys have to get off their butts and get fit. Good thing I'm not one of them."

Making a statement like this allows the team to discuss the matter openly. In this case, one of the girls might ask, "What do you think we can do about this, Coach?" This opens up a dialogue in which you can talk about fitness without pointing a finger at a particular group of players. It also allows the girls to make suggestions about fitness, which gives them a sense of control over the situation.

• Personal Feedback

Personal feedback is a little more difficult and probably even more important than team feedback. You have to address the player individually and look her in the eye to discuss her performance. If you're correcting an athlete on a particular play—"You made a pass here, when it should have gone over there"—that's technical feedback and it can be made in front of the team. But if you're coming down on a player, saying something like, "You're not playing at a level I know you can . . ." you should share the information in private.

You not only have to know what you're going to say to the player, but you must also understand its impact on that person. You can't just let her walk into your office and bluntly throw it out there for her without knowing what the repercussions of your message and style will be. You have to sit with it in your own mind for a second. Ask yourself, "I'm going to say this to her; how's she going to react?" This thoughtful, tempered and measured kind of feedback becomes much more effective because you end up filtering out things that may become negative to the whole relationship, ultimately sabotaging what you're trying to accomplish.

I know because I've made the mistake myself. I remember one time when I was coaching a player who was a fairly private woman. Throughout most of her college years she lived by herself. At some point I started to get feedback from her teammate/roommate that she wasn't a good roommate, that she was very demanding. One day I brought her into my office to talk about something else and then, without even thinking about it, I said, "What's going on with your roommate? She's complaining about you."

Almost immediately, I knew I'd made a mistake. And it was a big one. I should have said, "How are things going? You're doing well on the field, but how about off the field? Is the apartment all right? Are you enjoying your roommates?" That way, I could have heard her side of it without being confrontational. She might have said, "Well, there's a little bit of a clash. We're struggling, but I think we can work it out." But phrasing it the way I did was the worst thing I could have done. Before I opened my mouth, she didn't know anything about her roommate's complaints, and now she was completely on the defensive. My mistake cost me dearly. I had to rebuild the relationship and it took some time, including several apologies, before she was willing to open up to me.

Individual Meetings with Players

I'm a strong believer in having personal meetings with all my players, often just before a game. It allows me to give them some coaching advice and provides a chance for them to hear what is on my mind. Here's some advice for those personal meetings.

- Accept the fact that you can't solve the world's problems in one meeting. Zero in on one or two key ideas per meeting and leave it at that.
- Make sure you have positive comments because your players, no matter how secure you might think they are, are going to take some comments as personal assaults. I discovered this through coaching one of my sons when I used to ask, "Why do you have to do it this way?" He didn't hear that his soccer could be improved with a different way of doing something. He heard that as a person he wasn't good enough.
- Make sure you listen to what your player has to say. It can't be a monologue or a diatribe. It's a mutual discussion and some of the most effective sessions come when you invite the player's participation. If you listen, you may find out why your player is having a problem, providing you an opportunity to help her with it.
- Not every meeting has to be about the game. I've had meetings with players during which we wouldn't talk shop at all. I'd just ask them, "How's your mom and dad? I haven't seen them in a while." Or you might ask, "How's it going? Are you enjoying this experience?" Remember, you're dealing with young players and, for the most part, they're already hypercritical about every step they take. In our case, with the National Team, we had young players who were playing alongside players they wanted autographs from. Under those circumstances, the worst thing I could have done was try to micromanage what they were doing. Instead, I might ask them, "How does it feel to get a chance to play with some of the players you've been watching on television for years?" Or "What do you really love about being here?" "What scares you about being here?" These kinds of questions are likely

to get them to open up to you about their feelings and thoughts. They'll share what frightens them, what upsets them and what they're concerned about. And when they can communicate their issues, it helps to put players a little more at ease and creates a bond between you and your players.

The Halftime Talk

Halftime is a very critical point in the game. Over the years, I've listened to a countless number of halftime talks made by different coaches. Some were effective and productive, but others were just very overdone. Most often it's a time to point out things that are being done well and a few key points that can be improved.

My ritual after the end of the first half was to get together with my assistant coaches and, while the players were talking to each other, I'd spend five minutes or so asking my assistant coaches what they'd seen. Usually we'd come up with two or three offensive or defensive points that we wanted to address with the team. Even if there are more, and there certainly could be, it is best to limit them to no more than three items because you won't have the time to go over too many concerns. Also, your players can only absorb and focus on a few concepts as they start the second half. Remember, it's halftime; you must be specific and brief.

You also want to check on players who are playing with injuries or who may have other medical issues you need to be aware of. On the National Team, I had a wonderful medical staff and often would ask our trainer, Sue Hammond, or our regular doctors, Doug Brown or Mark Adams, prior to the halftime talk for an update on an injury or how a player was doing so I could formulate my second half lineup changes.

Some coaches yell at their players, and I have to admit I've sometimes done that. One instance that comes to mind occurred during halftime of the U.S./Germany game during the 1999 World Cup when we were losing 2–1 and Germany had just scored the go-ahead goal right before the half ended. I remember emphatically making one key point, which was, "If you want your dream to end here, today, keep doing what you're doing. I know you don't want that to happen, though, so here's what we need to do."

In my view, that halftime was my best in the tournament. It wasn't because I yelled but rather because I told the team what they needed to do. At the last moment, I kept from them one key piece of what we were going to do in the second half until we got back on the field. Then, seconds before the kickoff I got their attention. Only then did I give them the tactic, which was a certain high-energy defense I wanted them to play. We call it our 100 defense, which means 100 percent effort, 100 percent commitment and pressure over 100 percent of the field. I held it back because I knew that as soon as I told them, there would be an electrical charge associated with it. If I shared it with them in the locker room, the energy surge associated with the charge would have dissipated by the time they got out on the field.

So right before the kickoff, I yelled to Kristine Lilly, "One hundred!" I directed it to the right person because when Kristine turned around and yelled it to everyone else, they knew she was going to go after it. Collectively, as a unified team, we started off the second half very well and full of high energy. Actually, I didn't know if we had the energy to play a 100 defense, but I knew we had to go after it at that moment and hoped the emotions would carry us through. And they did. We came back and scored two more goals and won the game 3–2.

Although I try not to get too excited, I do think sometimes your personality has to come out a little bit. In fact, my players once told me, "It's okay if you yell at us," which I took as a sign of respect. They wanted to hear when I was angry because they felt that my anger mirrored their own disappointment in the way they were playing.

There are several important components to a productive halftime talk.

• The Emotion

You have to stir the players' emotions. At halftime during our game against China in the Olympics, I went into the locker room and said, "We have forty-five minutes to our dream. This is our dream and you guys have worked for it for a lifetime, and now we have forty-five more minutes to get it done." It was a measurable definition of what they had to do. I could almost hear the team thinking, "Oh God, it's only forty-five minutes . . . I can do forty-five minutes . . ." Rather than putting the outcome of a Gold Medal or the pressure of the Olympics in their heads, I used the idea that they had only forty-five minutes to go out and do what they had trained their whole lives to do. That tactic was specifically designed to appeal to their emotions.

- **Centering**

You want to help center the team so they'll focus on where they are and what has to be done. I would try to remind the team what they had already accomplished, saying things like, "This is an awesome event we're at, and you guys are playing some great soccer." I used this approach to bring them away from worry and fear and maybe even bring a smile to their faces. One of the many benefits to a smile is that it relaxes people. Even a sigh can produce feelings of calm and relaxation when it's combined with a deep, slow breath.

- **The Tactics**

After stirring their emotions and centering them, it's time to talk about game tactics. You might say something like, "We're in good shape. We're playing against a good team and they've scored a great goal. But we're okay if we do this and this and this. We can do it." Or sometimes you might be up by two or three goals and you can zero in on what the team has done wrong. *"We're up three goals, but our closing defense is awful. We can get better at that. So let's really go out and concentrate on when we close to make sure we're not just diving in. We want to close and contain and make it really difficult for that person to play."* If you give your team one behavior to focus on that's going to help maintain the intensity level, then you'll have more success than trying to overload them with too many concerns.

- **The Feedback**

There is such a thing as too much feedback and often halftime is when you should pull back a little in the total amount of feedback you give. If not, you run the risk of what is often termed paralysis by analysis. If you're constantly saying, "You've got to do this and this and this," well, after a while, the game becomes so complicated that you'll never get the desired result. Instead, zero in on one or two or three key points because that's the amount of information most players can process in such a short amount of time. If you don't, your team will reach a point where there's so much information coming at them that they won't be able to either remember it or apply it at all.

- Other Voices

If you're lucky enough to have assistant coaches, use them. When I was an assistant coach I often wanted an opportunity to say something, even if it was simply to say that I was enjoying the game. So when I became a head coach I would always give my assistant coaches a chance to say something during halftime. However, I limited it to only *one* thing. They might have felt there were other things to comment on, but they knew I only wanted them to contribute one key point.

A Coach's Checklist: How Am I Doing?

At certain points in the season it's a good idea to take stock of how you're doing as a coach. One would hope that a self-evaluation process is going on all the time, but whether it is or not I think that at some point near the beginning or middle of the season it's a good idea to complete some sort of self-examination as to how effective you are as a coach.

I always felt my team tested my abilities as a coach as much as I tested their abilities as players. I remember saying to them, "I hope you are as invested in improving your game as I am in improving my coaching. Because if you are, then we've got a lot of Gold Medals ahead of us." The message I was trying to send to them was, "Okay, I know how to coach, but that's not the end of the line for me." I was totally invested in becoming a *better* coach. I wanted them to know that, and I wanted them to emulate what I was trying to do by becoming better players.

I think the best way to evaluate your own performance as a coach is to ask yourself a series of questions:

- Do my players come to every practice excited and motivated to play? If they're having fun, they'll want to be there. If you're getting a lot of excuses about why they have to miss practice or if players are continually asking you what time it is, the chances are great that they're bored and they'd rather be someplace else.
- Do my players do their homework? If they come back the next day and show you the dribbling moves or the juggles that you demonstrated, then you know you've inspired them to go home and work on those moves in their backyards.
- Has my team shown any improvement? You should be able to assess your own performance by how well your team is developing. Compare where they were at the beginning of the season with how they're playing now, halfway into the season (you can also do this at the end of the season and, if you're doing a good job, you'll see an even more dramatic improvement).
- Is my team working as a unit? Are they interacting well with each other? If there's dissension or you're hearing a significant number of complaints, then it's time to reassess how effective your performance is as a coach.
- Are you having fun? It's almost impossible not to enjoy yourself if your players are enjoying themselves. Inevitably their joy will spill over to you and vice versa. If you're not having fun, chances are they aren't either.

If the answers to all these questions are yes, then no matter what your win-loss record is, you're doing a fine job that certainly bodes well for the rest of the season.

COLLEEN'S TEAM-BUILDING EXERCISES

Knots

Objective
To teach multidirectional communication and problem solving and demonstrate that communication never really ends.

Equipment
A long rope, depending upon size and number of players. With six or seven athletes the length of the rope should be half that of a basketball court, or 42 feet.

Number of Players
Teams of 6 to 7 per rope, maximum

Space
Any open space

The Game
Tie the same number of knots in the rope as there are participants. These knots should be evenly spaced along the full length of the rope. Each player is going to stand holding a knot with both hands on the rope. At that point each person must choose one hand that must never come off the rope. If it does, the whole team starts over again. The object is for one person at a time, in any order, to loosen the knot by using the one hand that can move. (Don't tell them which hand to use.) They then have to crawl through the opening of the loosened loop. The team wins when all six to seven people are standing with both hands on the rope and there are no more knots.

Debriefing
What did we learn from this exercise?
Why is it important to communicate?

What are some examples (positive and negative) where the content and tone of your teammates' communication influenced performance?

How would you do this activity differently next time?

How does this exercise relate to the game of soccer?

TONY'S CHALK TALK

Goalkeeping

Explanation

The goalkeeper position is a unique position in all of sport and I think goalkeepers are generally neglected. The necessary skills are vastly different from those of any other player on the team. Consequently, the challenge of working with the goalkeeper (one or two players) relative to working with all the other players (sixteen to eighteen) is apparent. The three methodologies for training a goalkeeper: coach-goalkeeper, coach-goalkeeper-players, and coach-goalkeeper-team.

1. Coach-goalkeeper: This is a one-on-one or one coach to two goalkeepers teaching situation, which must be done before or after practice. On the Women's National Team, the goalkeepers trained for 45 minutes before anyone else came out to practice.
2. Coach-goalkeeper-players: This is when a few players come out to train along with the goalkeepers. Because of the relationship of strikers trying to score and goalkeepers trying to save, exercises can be created that benefit both. This training is also done before or after practice. It was not uncommon for Danielle Fotopoulos or Cindy Parlow or Mia Hamm to come out early with the keepers.
3. Coach-goalkeeper-team: This is the methodology that most coaches have to utilize. Because they don't have the luxury of a goalkeeper coach or the ability to keep keepers after practice, they must use this methodology because it takes place during training with the entire team.

Exercise

During practice, the coach trains the goalkeepers while also creating an environment for all the field players. What the coach should not tell the field players is that the focus of this exercise is solely for the goalkeepers. But this exercise is really to benefit the goalkeepers and not the strikers or defenders. As coach, it's your job to facilitate the exercise so that the field players are doing it correctly, but your main objective is to coach only the goalkeepers.

The field size is approximately 36 to 40 yards long and 30 yards wide. There are large goals and a goalkeeper in each goal. Each team is positioned at its left goal post and each player has a ball. One team is designated to go first (team B). On the signal, the team B player sprints with the ball as in a breakaway toward team A's goal and tries to score. The team A goalkeeper tries to save. As soon as the ball is dead, which means there has been a score or a save or it's been knocked out of play, the first striker in line for team A starts out for team B's goal (at game speed) and the original striker from team B (the one who just tried to score) is the only defender. This repeats from side to side for 5 minutes and then scores are compared.

In this exercise, the field players are working on beating a defender or scoring with a defender by running stride by stride with her (as in a game) and the goalkeeper is making the decisions necessary to deal with a breakaway. At the same time the striker, who just had her scoring chance end, must immediately become a defender (this teaches the concept of transition).

There is one key rule: All strikers or field players try to score but must avoid contact with the goalkeeper. To make sure all the players understand, say it again because goalkeeper-field player contact has a real potential for injury. During your training sessions, you never want to encourage contact such as the breakaway type of contact that occurs when goalkeepers are diving at the striker's feet. This occurs when a goalkeeper on a breakaway dives across the path of the ball and the dribbler in order to protect the goal. These types of collisions are part of the game but can put players at risk. During training, I make a rule that there can be no contact with the goalkeeper during breakaway games. This rule protects both the goalkeeper and the field player.

Questions and Comments

What are the key coaching points for a goalkeeper?

As soon as a goalkeeper recognizes that there is a breakaway she has three options:

1. Win the ball before the shot is taken. This can happen when the striker overdribbles the ball so the key time to assess is on every touch by the striker.
2. Smother the shot. This happens when the striker and the goalkeeper arrive at the same time and, through courage and technique, the goalkeeper resolves the situation and smothers the shot. Please note in the above exercise, I have eliminated the smother option because I have asked that there be *no* contact.
3. Play the shot. This refers to the situation in which the striker has kept excellent control of the ball and there have been no opportunities for the keeper to win the ball before the shot. In this case the player must move away from the goal to cut down the angle (make the goal smaller). With good body position and body language she is saying to the striker, "Beat me if you can." Often the striker will beat the keeper and score, but if the keeper is in good position, she will force the striker to try to avoid her body. When that happens there is a good chance that the shot is saved or is hit wide.

How long should I stay in this exercise?

Not long. Remember, the goalkeeper is probably diving at 75 percent of the shots, so it's pretty demanding for her.

Coaching Challenge

When coaching the goalkeepers it is very easy to slip back into coaching the field players instead. Try to avoid that temptation and stay with your keepers. I say to the goalkeepers, "Okay, this exercise is for you. Let's work on coming out away from the goal and on taking space away from the striker as she approaches. Just make sure your body weight is forward and focus only on the ball. Let's play."

The other challenge is where you position yourself. Most coaches stay at the halfway line of the exercise and facilitate. If you are going to effectively coach your keeper, get back there with her and coach her from the goal area. Then move to the other goal or have the other goalkeeper change and come to the goal you are at so that you coach all the keepers, not just the starter.

CHAPTER 10

From Survive to Thrive

When you set a goal, write it down and then it's like making a promise to yourself.

—Tony DiCicco

Now that you're well into the season, you may find that it's more difficult to get your players motivated in practice or to listen to important coaching points. After all, they're more experienced now as players and probably think that practice and more coaching is the last thing they need. Don't be surprised if your practice sessions start to seem listless with your players simply going through the motions. It's not surprising. All too often people look at tasks in life as if they were on a giant "to do" list, and they rush through them simply so they can check them off and move on to the next one. This perspective is a mistake. Instead, they should be looking at tasks as opportunities to improve and it's your job as a coach to help teach players this lesson.

When Tiffeny Milbrett joined the Women's National Team, she had been a great scorer throughout her club and collegiate soccer career. But now she was entering a higher level of competition in which the goalkeepers were a little better, the defenders a little bit faster and the space a little tighter. Chances to score presented themselves less frequently and disappeared more quickly, so Tiffeny was not scoring the way she had at the lower levels.

Seeing her frustration, I took her aside one day and said, "First of all, Tiffeny, I want you to know that you *will* score at the international level because you are a special talent and because you've always scored with all the teams you've played for. You *will* get used to this level of play and you *will* score. We can do things that will help you adjust more quickly, however. For instance, when I give you time to shoot, instead of just shooting stationary balls in front of the goal, we're going to have somebody play balls to you where your back is to the goal and you'll have to turn and shoot them on goal."

In essence, what I was telling Tiffeny was that the quality of her practice was more important than the amount of time she spent on the field. More focus would be necessary and there would be greater demands placed on her to perform during practice. For her, practice would not be just a matter of going through the motions. She would now have very specific tasks that she would have to perform. These tasks were tailored to develop her strengths and help her raise the level of her game.

All great teams and all great athletes know how to train. They know how to use time in order to gain a competitive advantage. They realize that it isn't just a matter of quantity but of quality of practice. They know how to maximize the time they have, using it to perfect those parts of their game that need perfection or to improve those parts of their game in which there's room for improvement. Essentially, great athletes always want to be better. And, more important, they truly believe that they *can* get better. They are never satisfied with where they are and are constantly demanding higher levels of performance from themselves. These players don't just get done with practice, they get better with practice. They have an ability for self-analysis and they have a vision of what they want for themselves, a vision that motivates them toward greater levels of achievement.

We tried to instill this principle in our team, which meant we had to challenge players to compete against themselves and against their own previous best performances. We wanted them to constantly raise the bar of excellence within themselves. But could we implement this competitive challenge by training at higher levels of intensity? Could we expect higher concentration levels? We felt we could and, as a result, our training sessions were incredibly intense. I got a kick out of the press reaction when we started to split up the World Cup champions into eight teams for the professional league, the WUSA. Reporters would come to me and ask, "How can they compete against each other? They're so close, they're like sisters. How are they going to compete against each other?" I would just laugh and say, "Have you ever been to one of our practices? Have you ever seen these players play 4v4, like it was the last game in their career?" It's just the way they played: They didn't just get it done, they trained to get better. And I think that's something you can instill in your team as well as in your individual players. It's part of the culture you build into your team.

Setting a team challenge involves getting your team together and saying something like, "Occasionally, we're going to have bad days. We're all going to make bad plays from time to time. There are going to be days where you're carrying your teammate, and you need to do it because she's struggling. And then there are going to be days when she's carrying you, and she needs to because you're struggling. But you never, ever give up. That's the way successful teams behave."

This doesn't mean, however, that training can't be fun. Clearly, it *must* be fun, and one of the jobs of the coach is to make it fun and keep it fun. It certainly was for us. During the breaks in our training sessions, when the players would go over to get a drink, they'd be razzing each other, they'd be laughing, they'd be giggling. But make no mistake about it, when it was time to walk back out on the field, they'd be ready to go. "What's the next exercise, Coach? Challenge me, Coach, because I want to evolve as a player and I want to win at that level." And the result was that, as a team, we were able to develop a we-know-how-to-win, we'll-find-a-way-to-win mentality.

Setting Training Goals

Before each training session I would meet with my staff and we'd ask ourselves, "What do we want from this training session?" And we would first set the rhythm of the session, which was often dictated by the kind of playing schedule we had. For instance, in the 1996 Olympics the format was day 1, a game; day 2, rest and travel; day 3, a game; day 4, rest and travel; day 5, a game. So during that period, that would be the rhythm we created in our training regime. When we trained on Monday, it was hard; on Tuesday it was moderate or light. Wednesday was hard; Thursday was moderate to light. It was the same rhythm we would experience in the Olympic tournament. In the World Cup of 1999 we had a game on day 1; days 2 and 3 would be for rest and travel, and day 4 would be another game, so it was a different rhythm. As a result, our training matched that rhythm. Of course, if you're playing at a recreational level where you have a practice or two and a game all within a week, you'll have to adjust the schedule accordingly. For instance, if you have practices Tuesdays and Thursdays and games on Saturdays or Sundays, then your Tuesday practice may be light and your Thursday practice somewhat harder.

As a coach it's your job to create the focus of a given training session. Ideally, you have to create a challenge for your players to survive and to thrive. You must progressively build the challenge, and you must also guide your players to success in meeting that challenge. You might say to the team, "Your challenge today is concentration because we're doing tactical training. It's not going to be a lot of physical work, but you must concentrate because we're going to talk about how our defense shifts . . ."

As always, be sure to make these challenges no longer than ten minutes or so. Sometimes coaches will stay on one training exercise for forty-five minutes and then they lose their team mentally and emotionally. Don't be afraid to invent exercises that are tailored to a particular problem. In our team meetings we'd say, "We want to accomplish these three outcomes from this exercise." For instance, if we were playing Norway (a team known for flighting balls or kicking long ball passes that create heading duels), I might say something like, "Okay, we've got to practice combative heading, so let's come up with an exercise on that that's fun."

What to Do if Someone Isn't Going All Out

Sometimes you're going to find a player dogging it in practice or in a game. If that happens, the best thing to do is pull the player aside and be specific as to what you want. "Listen, you need to be fully in or completely out of the game. If you're going to stay in, here's what you need to do. You need to make runs into the flank because that's the only place you can possibly get the ball." Or "I need you to close down this player. Just jogging to the player and letting her serve out of your area doesn't mean you're playing defense. You need to show me that you can prevent service from your zone. If you can do these things, you're going to be a better player and we're going to be a better team."

Using Competition to Get Better

I used competition in almost everything we did, but there always had to be an element of fun and excitement to it as well. A simple power-heading exercise might involve my serving a ball to a player for her to head as far back as she could. Adding an element of competition to it would involve seeing who on the team could hit it farthest. The way I created even more competition was to split the group into two teams and create what I call a moving net. There were two teams of four or five players and I tossed the ball to one of them, and they headed it as far as they could. When it hit the ground, the imaginary net moved to where the ball hit the ground. Then the other team tried to head it farther, creating another line closer to their opponent's goal. Each team tried to get the ball over their opponent's goal line and the net moved back and forth, depending on team performance. You can even make it more interesting by adding five-yard penalties for when the ball goes out of bounds.

We'd also play a 1v1 game where one team lined up at the right post and they would try to score on the other goal, thirty or so yards away, while the other team was lined up at the right post, trying to score on the other goal. The first team took their turn and as soon as that ball was dead, the other team started, with each team trying to score the most goals while the two goalkeepers competed against each other to stop them. The key component was that as soon as a player attempted to score and her ball was dead, she became the defender and was chasing or closing the other team's attacker, the one who broke toward the goal on the "dead ball, out of play" cue. I could have these field players, five or six in each line, doing all these breakaways, scoring, while the primary focus of the exercise was for the goalkeeper to practice saves. It didn't matter because it was a competition, and both the goalkeepers and the field players would play hard.

Another technique you can incorporate to engender competition is to have a mini-elimination tournament. For instance, we'd have a 4v4 tournament, just like in the World Cup group play when only the top two teams go to the medal round. So in our miniround-robin tournament, only the top two teams played in the "championship" game, while the other two teams had to watch. Being a spectator was hard for these competitive players and they'd ask me, "Tony, can't we play for third place?" And on occasion we did, but most often my answer was, "No, because in the real world only two teams go through to the medal round, so you're watching." And so they would do anything to win because the worst thing these competitors could do was to sit and watch their teammates play.

After a while, competition becomes a way of life. Our players were competitive in practically everything they did, whether it was horseshoes, cards or tiddledywinks. They obviously cared about each other, but at the same time they weren't about to give an inch in terms of competitiveness. I remember one day when I asked two separate groups of players to move the goals closer together. One group went north, the other south. At first they started walking the goals toward each other, but it wasn't long before they were trotting and then finally running toward the respective spots, trying to beat the other group. They just couldn't stop themselves from competing, even when it came to moving the practice goals.

Remember, though, whatever you do, keep it fun, keep it realistic and keep it competitive. This means that you should approximate in practice conditions that are as similar as possible to the game itself. I firmly believe that my coaching record of 103–8–8 can be credited to our players always training as if they were in a real match. When they competed in games, they only knew maximum effort because they duplicated match conditions every day in training.

COLLEEN'S TEAM-BUILDING EXERCISES

Scavenger Hunt

Objective

To generate your own challenge and your own competition and to work cooperatively with a teammate. You can merely go through the motions, making it appear as if you're scavenging, and get the job done, but we're not just trying to get it done; we really want to do this exercise as best and as fast as we can. The goal is to challenge ourselves with competitive demands.

Equipment

The scavenger hunt list with 15 to 25 items written (one per line). Make a box or line next to the item so that the "judge" or "referee" can check items off as completed, once players feel they have been successful. The 15 to 20 items that you've hidden for the players to find, some examples include a feather, a 1986 penny, an egg shell, a green stick, a copy of the team's schedule, the title of the third song on some group's CD or tape, a straw, a business card from someone you don't know, a rock shaped like a triangle, a red rubber band.

The Game

The idea is to learn how to work together as a team. To increase the opportunities for dialogue, problem solving, frustration control and creativity, I like to have athletes placed in groups of two, three or four players forming a single team. They can decide to work as a group the entire time or split up and then divide and conquer, so to speak, thus adding a tactical and strategic component to the game.

The Hunt

Give your athletes a time limit, for example, thirty minutes to get as many items as they can. The winning team is the one with the most items from the list in the shortest possible time. Another method of scoring would be to divide your group into two teams of equal numbers with the winning team securing every item on the scavenger list in the shortest time possible.

Develop your scavenger list with the age, safety concerns, distance traveled, object availability and level of difficulty you believe appropriate for your team.

As soon as all teams receive the list, the clock starts and off the teams go, each trying to scavenge items from the list.

Debriefing

When were you excited and motivated in your scavenger activity?
    When were you passive, worried or apprehensive?
What approaches did the most successful groups use? The least
    successful?
Does luck play a role in the success of this activity? If so, how?
Did you enjoy the process of finding items on the list, or were you
    only motivated when you were successful?
How does this challenge relate to the game of soccer?

TONY'S CHALK TALK

Shooting and Scoring

Every player on the field should become comfortable in front of goal when confronted with a scoring opportunity. Some will be more comfortable than others and those are your forwards. This is an exercise that allows everyone the opportunity to score or assist on goals.

Exercise

The field size is 36 yards long (two penalty areas together) by 44 yards wide. Create two teams with eight players on each side. Use regulation goals and goalkeepers. Each team starts with four players on the field and four players (two per side) on the touch lines (sidelines). If you have extra players (one or two), they can be plus players. Plus players are players who play offense with the team in possession of the ball. They don't play defense, so the attacking team always has a numerical advantage, which should result in more shooting and scoring. The players on the touch lines are also part of the game; they have one or two touches, so a teammate from inside the game can pass them the ball and they can cross a ball in front of the opponent's goal or make a pass to set up a shot. (Keep touch-line players alert; don't let them become spectators in the game.) Play for 5 minutes, then switch the players on the touch line with the players in the game.

Be creative with your rules. For instance, perhaps a head goal can be worth 2 points.

Questions and Comments

What do I emphasize in the exercise?

Shooting is the first key element. Everyone should look to shoot. The field is short, so if your players are at half field they are only 18 yards away from their opponent's goal. Teach your players that the difference between shooting and scoring is like the difference between a baseball pitcher's throwing and pitching. A shooter just winds up and hits it hard every time; a scorer sees what is available and then shoots. Sometimes, she will pass the ball into the back of the net, sometimes she will strike it as hard as possible. The best forwards learn how to bend the ball around defenders and goalkeepers or chip or dribble the ball around goalkeepers.

How do I keep the players on the touch line engaged?

Allow them to take two touches. Their first touch can bring them onto the field of play. From there, they can do more damage and even shoot the ball themselves. This is not only good for shooting and scoring, but it's also a lot of fun. A maximum of 15 or 20 minutes should allow plenty of time for player development.

Coaching Challenge

Keep play stoppages to a minimum, but keep mental or written notes about coaching points you can teach with a different exercise on a different day.

CHAPTER 11

Failure as Fertilizer

Placing blame on others is easy. Taking responsibility for yourself is empowering.

— Tony DiCicco

One of the toughest things a coach and a team have to deal with is losing. Losses are inevitable, but that doesn't make them any easier to take. Even the best teams lose and even the best players make errors, both physical and mental. Think about it. In baseball the batting champion usually hits in the low or mid three hundreds. That means more than two-thirds of the time he's making an out. That batter is failing. Thomas Edison discovered 1,999 ways that light bulbs didn't work, but those failures were necessary for him to discover the one way that they did work. When viewed this way, failures can be viewed as fertilizer because they help ready us for growth and future possibilities.

When I took over the team in the summer of 1994, we were already World Champions and we were preparing to defend our title in Sweden the next year. Unfortunately, the following summer at the 1995 World Cup in Sweden, we lost to Norway in the semifinals and they went on to win the tournament. Yet there were major consequences from that loss and each of these made us a stronger team, illustrating the concept Colleen calls failure as fertilizer.

First of all, there was no finger pointing within the team after we lost. Nobody said, "DiCicco didn't substitute properly or he played the wrong system," although I personally felt that my coaching lacked something. Nobody said, "Mia Hamm didn't score a goal." Or "Briana Scurry allowed a goal to be scored; she needed to make that save." There was none of that, which was very positive. The second consequence was that everybody looked inside themselves, as did I, and said things like, "You know, I could have done a better job out there on the field." Or, in my case, "I could have coached better." Each and every one of our players said, "I could have been a better player. I should have performed at a higher level. I let the team down. I could have been more prepared." This attitude led to a saying that we used during preparation for the 1996 Olympics, which was, "I could have been better. I *will* be better."

Something else came out of that loss to Norway that wound up becoming an important rallying cry for us. After they'd won, the Norwegians, in celebration, performed a unified train crawl. The players knelt down on the field on all fours and each player behind grabbed the ankles of the player in front. It was probably a very genuine expression of their elation at winning: I don't really think they were doing it to denigrate out team, but most of our players perceived it as an in-your-face gesture, and it was an image that would stay with us for some time, a reminder, of sorts, of what it felt like to lose. In a strange way, that train crawl by the Norwegian team was the beginning of our preparation for the 1996 Olympics. But there was more to the story.

After we lost in the semifinals and were eliminated from the tournament, the pain of unfulfilled expectations began to sink in. As the championship game day approached, a number of players came up to me and said, "Tony, do we have to go watch the finals?" I didn't hesitate. "Yes, we have to go to the finals." I had a good reason. I wanted them to be there and *not* be in the game because I knew that would serve as motivation in the future. So we all went to the finals and, of course, it was a very empty feeling watching two teams compete for the trophy that we wanted so badly.

After the game was over, the players asked me, "Do we have to go to the postgame banquet?" Again I didn't hesitate. "Yes, we have to go to the banquet," which, incidentally, was held in the same beautiful old Swedish hall where the Nobel Prize ceremony is held.

It was in this austere, historical setting that Michelle Akers and Carin Gabarra had to relinquish their trophies from 1991, and it was here that the Golden Ball, given to the best player in the tournament, and the Golden Boot, presented to the high scorer, were awarded to the Norwegian players.

During the post–World Cup banquet, the FIFA press officer stated, as he was acknowledging the Norwegian champions, "Certainly, in our sport, we have never seen such beautiful champions!" He wasn't saying it to put the Americans down, but that kind of sentiment was just one indication of how winners—at least by the scoreboard—are treated in comparison to those who fail. When we didn't win, we were, for all intents and purposes, invisible. Of course when the press officer realized what he'd said, he approached the team to apologize. Carla Overbeck, always classy, just said, "Don't worry about it, we were not offended." But in reality the players were very upset.

On the bus ride back, I spoke to the team and made reference to that statement offered by the press officer. "You know, the margin on the field between winning and losing was laser thin. In fact, we hit the crossbar twice in the closing minutes of that 1–0 loss to Norway. The margin on and off the field, between being champions, being revered and coming in second or third is enormous. We were at the banquet for two hours, but in essence, we were invisible. We did not exist. Only Norway existed. And I want you to remember that difference."

That little speech on the bus must have hit home. During the process of building the team for the 1996 Olympics, we knew that we were no longer the best team in the world. We knew we were no longer World Champions. And that fact motivated us. That failure to win became the fertilizer we needed to perform at the highest level the next time we got the chance.

There was, of course, another way I could have handled the situation, but I think it would have been a big mistake. I could have noted all the external reasons why we lost. "We didn't get a chance to practice on the field the night before because it rained." Or "We did all the traveling in this event, which included two nine-hour train rides because of the airline strike in Sweden during the World

Cup." But I think one of the qualities I have, and one that was shared by the team, is that I can be an objective and fairly accurate evaluator of myself and the team. And my evaluation was that the best team won in 1995. Once you come to that objective realization and don't blame your loss on the referee or the excessive travel or the field conditions, you can then focus and deal with what you have to do to make yourself and your team better. You can begin to create a plan, a training environment and a vision so that the next time you play you're the winner, standing on that top podium receiving the Gold Medal. The key is to focus your energies on the factors and variables that are under your control as a player, as a coach and as a team. At that point, and only at that point, can you start asking the right questions, which begin with, "How do we become the best team in the world again?" "What do I need to do to become a better player?" "How do I improve as a coach?" If you ask things like, "Why did we have to do all the traveling?" you will get lots of answers but they won't be the correct or the most helpful or productive ones.

And so, as we moved into 1995 and started to prepare for the Olympics in Atlanta, *it* was always there. And what I mean by "it," and the players knew exactly what I meant, was our loss to Norway. *It* was always with us. *It* is still with me today. *It* made me a better person, and *it* certainly made me a better coach—and without question *it* made us a better team. Whatever it was that we needed— that extra motivation for an extra practice, or understanding why Coach is running this fitness routine, or why we need to have a team meeting—*it* was always there. *It* was in every training session. *It* was in every friendly game we played. *It* was in every fitness session. *It* was in every tournament. *It* was always in the back of our minds—that loss, and the feeling surrounding that loss to Norway. And *it* was tremendous motivation.

It even took on a very concrete form for me as coach. In our preparation for the Olympics and beyond, I had a photograph of Norway as champions that I would post so the team could see it. Because if anything ever epitomized failure as fertilizer, it was that game, and that loss. Some of the players even posted photographs of Norway holding the World Cup trophy by their front doors so that every time they left for practice, they'd see that photo. Often they'd tap the wall or the picture and vow, "Never again. Next time it's ours!" Today, seven years later, I still carry the photograph showing Norway receiving the World Cup trophy.

In our case, losing that game became everyone's internal motivator to push harder. And what was amazing was that in 1996 we played the same outstanding Norwegian team and we outshot them 28–8 in the Olympic semifinal. We won the game in golden goal, extra time, but when we walked off the field, I knew we were the better team. And in the press conference, sitting next to the Norwegian coach, when I was asked about the game, I said, "They're always difficult wins. But in 1995, Norway won. They were the better team and deserved to win. Today we won. We were the better team. We deserved to win." And when the press turned to the Norwegian coach and asked what he thought, he said simply, "I concur."

Many of the players had their own personal instances of failure as fertilizer that they drew on. For example, Brandi Chastain had been a reserve player on the 1991 World Cup squad, but when the team started to reorganize in 1993, Anson Dorrance, then the head coach, didn't invite Brandi back, effectively cutting her. She was devastated, and she eventually went over to Japan to play in the Japanese league. In 1995 she was not a member of the World Cup team. So basically, between 1991 and 1995, she was not involved with the Women's National Team as an active player. She did attend one or two camps, but she really didn't perform that well. After we lost in 1995, Brandi called me up and she said she wanted a tryout. She promised she'd come into camp in shape, and she wanted to show me that I needed her on the team. I said, "Okay." She came in September of 1995, just a couple months after we'd been eliminated by Norway and were starting over and beginning to prepare for the 1996 Olympics. Her play was outstanding. A couple of months later I brought her back for our second training camp, and again she played outstandingly. "Brandi," I explained to her, "here's the situation. You've been one of our best players in training camp. I want you to be on the residency team (the team that would move to Florida together). I think you have a chance to start if you're willing to change your position."

"I just want to play anywhere," Brandi said. And so, even though she'd always been an attacking player, she became a defender. She played so well that she became a starter, and a key player for the National Team that went on to win the Gold Medal. Today, behind Mia Hamm, she's probably the best known woman player in America and a sports icon in her own right. This is a tremendous success story that started with failure. Just think how many times she probably thought, "Oh, just give it up." But she didn't. She used that failure to motivate herself toward success again, turning her failure into fertilizer.

Another example of this principle is the case of Shannon MacMillan. Shannon finished her collegiate career in the fall of 1995, having won most of the collegiate honors: best player; the Herman trophy, the soccer equivalent of the Heisman trophy; and the MAC trophy, from the Missouri Athletic Conference, which is presented to the country's best player. That December, I had her come into camp and try out for the residency team that would prepare for the Olympics. She was actually on the roster but was taken off just before it was posted. She was the last person who didn't make the final cut. I loved her as a player, but it was just a numbers game. We were only allowed a specific number of players on our roster and someone had to be eliminated.

So Shannon, after winning all those collegiate awards just weeks before, and being at the peak of her game, left that camp totally devastated. She thought her career was over. After all, there weren't many other teams she could play for—this was *the* team. But to her credit she didn't give up. And she didn't hang up on me the next time I called her, which happened to be a few weeks later when our National Team players were having a contract issue with the U.S. Soccer Federation. Some of them could not make a trip to South America because of a boycott. Suddenly, a few roster possibilities opened up. I called Shannon and said, "Shannon, I know this is last minute. We're going to Brazil. Do you want to come?" Without hesitation she said yes.

Shannon came to Brazil and I saw that I'd made a mistake by not keeping her. I literally created an extra spot for her on the team going into residency, and she went on to become our leading scorer in the Olympics. The fact that she failed to make the team actually seemed to maker her hungrier and more determined.

Extracting the Lessons from Failure

I don't know if you can actually teach someone to be as tenacious and directed as Shannon and Brandi are, but you can guide them in a healthy direction. After Brandi was cut, she felt her life was shattered. She'd just been eliminated from the team and wondered what should she do. Brandi could have thrown her ball and her shoes in the closet and felt sorry her herself. She could have said, "How could he do this to me?" But that would have made her a victim and whenever you feel like a victim, the first question you have to ask yourself is: "How did I make it easy for this to happen?" That question puts the onus back on you at some level. You acknowledge you had some responsibility in what happened to you and just by doing that, you start to take control of what will happen in the future.

Luckily, and happily for Brandi and Shannon, they chose options that made future greatness possible. They took responsibility for their setbacks and took action to change. They understood that, in fact, it was really an imposed failure: They didn't *fail:* Failure was projected onto them by somebody else who was making the decisions. For Brandi it was Anson and for Shannon it was I. At some level they had failed to impress the coach enough. On another level, *they* didn't fail: The coach failed to recognize their potential, and it took *their* ability to change a negative into a positive to make the key difference. They said to themselves, "I'm going to prove to the coach that he is wrong. I'm going to work hard, stay positive, and look for that next opportunity." And when the next opportunity came, they made the best of it.

Colleen always encouraged players to extract the meaningful lessons. Extract what you can and then discard the rest and go onward with what you've learned. It's not easy. It's so much easier just to sulk, feel sorry for yourself, hide or to say, "How could this person do this to me? This shouldn't have happened to me." That's the easy route to take. Instead, you have to learn to use failure and turn it into motivation, into a lesson that's going to make you a better performer the next time an evaluation comes up.

A coach, parent or teacher can guide that process. I teach what I call the twenty-four-hour rule. For the next twenty-four hours you can feel sorry for yourself, you can sulk, you can stay in bed the whole time. But twenty-four hours and one minute from now, I want you up and thinking about what you're going to do to correct whatever the problem is. You're going to be sad for a while—that's natural—but it's not acceptable to be sad indefinitely, or to allow the sadness to stop you from functioning. You extract what you can from the experience and then move on.

Colleen was wonderful in working with the players in these situations. The players had such trust in her that they would buy into where she was leading them, and she was invaluable in getting players to use failure as fertilizer. But it wasn't just the players. Colleen was also able to show me how my failures could be turned around and used as fertilizer for success.

For instance, one day I really lost it emotionally and lashed out verbally at Shannon in practice. From my perspective, I had a player who was an incredible talent, who was awesome in the Olympics, and then in the spring of 1997, during our victory tour, she was injured. She didn't come back until some point in 1998, and she wasn't the same player on the field. She was healthy and could have been as good as she had been before, but she just wasn't performing with the same vigor, energy and sharpness. My goal was to bring her back to her full form for the World Cup.

It was a more difficult task than I thought it would be. She had so many physical and technical talents, and her skill level was incredibly high, but something was holding her back. And so, one day my frustrations just got the best of me. On the day after a game, the players who played a lot of minutes can just jog and stretch, but the other team members play against each other. The staff also jumps into those games and plays. On this day, I purposely matched myself up against Shannon, and I said to her, "I want you to beat me every time. I want you to dribble past me. I want you to score goals on me. I want you to take me to the cleaners. I'm going to try to stop you, but you're good enough to be able to beat me." Fifteen minutes in, I was the better player. Thirty minutes in, she still hadn't done anything spectacular. I'd totally shut her down and I was contributing more to my team than she was to hers. Now I was not only upset and frustrated, I was also angry. We needed her and she was just not giving her team what she had. So, toward the end of the practice game, I started to bait her into an argument. I wanted to have it out with her. I wanted to let her know that she was not getting it done, that she didn't have the heart to get it done. To her credit, she wouldn't engage me in the argument.

So it became something of a one-sided argument with a ranting lunatic—unfortunately, me—and a quiet, underperforming player. When the scrimmage was over, I just stormed off the field. It didn't take long for me to realize what I'd done. I'd crossed a line. I'd tried to bait a player into an argument—and I felt awful. I felt like I'd lost my composure and my ability to influence this player the way I'd hoped. Worse yet, I had done so in front of all her teammates. I felt as if I'd lost my team's respect. I'd had an emotional outburst and now I was sitting on the picnic bench waiting for the team to come up to the bus, and I was really at a loss.

Finally, Mia Hamm came up to me and asked, "Are you all right?"

"I don't know, Mia. I think I really crossed a line. And I feel awful." We talked for a couple of minutes and then we got on the bus and, as we drove back to the hotel, I knew I had to apologize, and I had to do it in front of everyone else. And so, when the bus stopped, I stood up and turned around and, with some luck, my eyes caught Shannon's and I said, "I need to apologize and I need to do it in front of everyone. I need you to hear me say that I don't know why I did that—I know I crossed a line. I have no excuse for it, Shannon, and I am sincerely sorry."

And that, I was hoping, was the end of it—at least I thought it was the end of it. But within the next hour or two a couple of players knocked on my door, and others sent e-mails that I read later in the evening—all in one way or another thanking me. I think they realized that I'd had to become very vulnerable to apologize in front of everyone. And when I did it, the team was relieved because they knew that everything was okay. In fact, in some ways, we were even stronger as a group.

I saw this as a failure on my part—losing my temper, allowing my frustration to get the better of me—but Colleen saw it differently. She looked at it as an extraordinary teachable moment and a lesson for the team. It showed the players that the head coach, the number-one leader, could make a mistake and could fail. They saw me take responsibility and move on. So, even if it wasn't deliberate, it planted another seed. It sent the message that when the players make mistakes on the field, it's okay as long as they learn from them and become stronger. I'd made a mistake, and I'd apologized for it. And so Colleen, in her infinite wisdom, put a positive twist on what in my eyes was still a huge blunder.

Certainly, anybody who fails time after time after time is going to have confidence challenges, so the trick is to put yourself in an environment where you can be successful. And it's important to remember that failing is a necessary ingredient to ultimate success. I knew it as a goalkeeper and I know it as a coach. Until you fail and learn how to deal with failure, you cannot fully succeed. People look at failure as something to be avoided or to feel embarrassed about, or as some depressing event in life's journey. Although, obviously, one should not try to fail, it's not a disaster if one does. Instead, it's an opportunity to learn and then use the lessons to become stronger. Failure is essential for advancement, achievement and success. And this advice is coming from someone who used to want to play perfect games, who had a lot of trouble dealing with the imperfect games. I had to learn to use failure to become what I'd call a professional. In my view you're not a professional unless you're willing to take risk to the point of failure, and you're not a professional unless you know how to productively use failure when it happens. The goal is to extract the relevant lessons. What have I learned? How can I use it to my advantage? Why am I different because of this experience?

COLLEEN'S TEAM-BUILDING EXERCISES

Wrong-Way Wiffle Ball

Objective

To layer peak performance strategies into everything the players do, including training sessions and competitive games. As a sport psychology consultant, I provide outlines of principles and techniques to the players as a group and then follow up with the athletes individually.

In terms of failure as fertilizer, I advise players about a three-part reframing process (adapted from Kirschenbaum) they can use after failing or making errors, which is termed the three Fs: Fudge, Fix and Focus

1. **Fudge:** When there is an error, the player first reacts with, "Oh, that's a bummer!" Or maybe she says the word "fudge." It never feels good to make an error, so the first thing the player needs to do is to acknowledge it emotionally.
2. **Fix:** Often, the first emotionally based reaction is an automatic response, usually anger, frustration, disappointment or fear. But a player can't let herself get stuck in that emotional phase. The next step, which requires thought, practice and effort, is to progress forward to task-oriented thinking. The athlete learns to ask herself: What was the error? What should I have done? What can I do now? This is rational analysis.
3. **Focus:** There are only three points in time for an athlete: past, present and future. Wherever you focus, that's where your energy goes. Does it do any good to focus in the past or in the future? No. The focus must be in the here and now. So the final step is the combination of a focus or cue word to bring the person back to the immediate performance. The focus should be on this play, this moment. It's right-now thinking and awareness. That's where maximum control is for athletes: Right now!

Here's a concrete illustration you can use to show your group how this process works in reality. Perhaps a player missed a shot on what clearly should have been a goal-scoring opportunity. Of course that's disappointing. Of course the player made an upsetting mistake and so her first reaction is to acknowledge it and take responsibility for it. So the fudge portion becomes, "Doggone it, I blew it." But very quickly the player has to analyze the reason for the error and attempt to fix it. In this case, she may say, "I have to keep my head down and knee over the ball longer. That will help keep my shot low and on the goal frame." Then, the final step is to focus on the present. Focus on this play, this moment and this particular game responsibility. Players can't perform when their attention is focused on the past or the future. So the player now focuses on hustling back to the proper defensive position to try to win the goal kick being sent by the keeper.

Wrong-way Wiffle ball is an exercise that will have your team dealing with and learning from failure while also having a lot of fun.

Equipment
Wiffle bat, Wiffle ball, and four bases.

Number of Players
Two teams of 6 to 10 players.

Space
Large enough for a small- to medium-size softball field.

The Game
Most softball rules apply, although the game is played backward. In each inning, everyone on the team bats once. The other team is in the field. People pitch to their own team. You must bat on your nondominant side (that is, lefties bat righty and vice versa). Batters run the opposite way, to third instead of first, and continue around the bases in that direction. You can accumulate people on bases, that is, more than one player on a base at a time. A fly ball is an out. A ground ball must be touched by everyone on the fielding team before they try to get the opposing player out. In other words, if

the ball is hit toward the third base, everyone on the team would run to that spot. The ball would then be fielded and touched by everyone on the team before the attempt to get the runner out. You may only throw the ball with your nondominant arm. Runners may keep going around the bases until they are stopped at one or are tagged out. You may round the bases as many times as you can. The team that scores the most runs wins the game. Adjust the number of innings played to the interest of your players and the time available.

Lesson

This game is fraught with failure. Runners forget to run or they run the wrong way. Fielders forget to touch the ball or they throw it to the wrong base with the wrong arm. But as the game goes on, players learn from their mistakes and they improve. The lesson? If you're demoralized, you're done. If you stick with it, failure can eventually breed success.

Debriefing

What does this game tell you about failure?

How did you react to your teammates when they did things incorrectly?

How did you react when you made an error?

Can you be successful sometimes even when you do things the wrong way?

How does this game pertain to your team this season?

TONY'S CHALK TALK

Defending

Generally, when a coach refers to defending in soccer he or she has to address which third of the field the players are defending. Is it the defensive third, the midfield third or the attacking third? Is it player-to-player defending or is it zone defending? For the purpose of this exercise, I suggest you consider building the overall knowledge of defending, which includes individual and zonal defending challenges.

Exercise
Create two teams of five players each. If you have twenty players, you can set up two games, but make sure there is adequate space between the two games so there is no chance of injuries. If you have fewer than twenty players, then just substitute players on a regular basis.

Each team has two defenders and two attackers and they must play within their own halves of the field. There is also a plus player for each half of the field. The plus player will play with the attack when they have possession and play with the defenders when they have possession. The size of the field can be adjusted, depending on the ability level of the defenders, but start at 50 yards long (two halves of 25 yards) and 30 yards wide. Each team attacks two goals that have been placed on the goal lines, approximately 5 yards from each corner. Remember, you are working with the defenders for both teams, so don't spend much time at all on coaching the attack.

Questions and Comments

What are the key coaching points of this exercise?
Defensive communication and organization. The player who closes (that is, closes the space and puts defensive pressure on the ball) the ball, must communicate with the other defender, who pro-

vides cover (slightly at an angle and behind the first defender). If the cover defender moves over too far, the goal on the other side of the field will be left open. If the cover defender doesn't provide enough cover, then the attack (remember, it's 3v2 due to the plus player) will exploit the numerical advantage and attack the goal of the first defender.

One lesson inherent in this exercise is for players to learn that they can't dive in without measuring the consequences. This means that they shouldn't go for the steal unless they are sure they can make it because if they miss, they will have two goals to attack and only one defender to defend.

Coaching Challenge

Adjust the size of the field so that the defenders are challenged yet have enough success to build confidence. As you start to add numbers you may also increase the size of the field. When you get to a full field situation, then you may have four defenders with three goals across the field to defend. The final stage is to build to a full game by bringing in the goalkeeper. Remember, coach what you can use to get improvement in your players, but also catch them being good!

CHAPTER 12

Act *As If*

Talent is not enough. It's an important component in a successful performance, but it's really only a starting point.

— TONY DICICCO

There is a certain point in any season when attitude, and not simply talent, plays a large part in whether your team wins or loses. Attitude is a choice that can color any situation, and attitude, whether it reflects confidence or lack of it, is contagious. In effect, you've got to get your players to talk the talk and walk the walk. You must encourage them to act *as if* they are the players they want to be, the players they admire.

At first, attitude is almost always internal. It's all about how your body and psyche read the information coming from your brain. If I walk into an auditorium to make a speech as if I don't think I belong there, the chances are that that's the kind of energy that will flow into my words. Conversely, if I walk in there, despite how intimidating it may be, as if I'm going to impart a wisdom that has great meaning, and that I'm going to do it successfully, then I increase the likelihood that I'm going to present myself as somebody who has something important to say. On the field, body language speaks volumes. When people see us bent over, with heads down, we look tired or undermotivated and, as a result, vulnerable. On the other hand, if we walk with a crispness in our step, our eyes up, people will assume that this is how we feel and they will respond to us accordingly.

A good part of successful performance is learning to manipulate your presentational skills. Players may not feel confident, but they need to take on the appearance of confidence. The team may not feel like champions yet, but the key is the word "yet." ("We haven't won yet, but we will.")

Needless to say, confidence is incredibly important to the concept of acting *as if.* The coach and the players must act *as if* they can handle every situation, and by that I don't mean being cocky. And I'm not saying you have to use Mohammed Ali's level of verbiage. You do, however, have to act *as if* you know what it takes to get the job done. If you can successfully communicate this attitude to your inner psyche, then you can be prepared for whatever comes your way. For example, when professional players miss kicks or blow layups in basketball, they run down the field or court with no visible sign to indicate that they've just made a key mistake. On the other hand, if a young player misses a shot you can often see her beating herself up all the way back down the field or court, perhaps while shaking her head or making arm gestures of anger or disbelief. A professional player is saying, "I can make that shot and I *will* make it the next time." The amateur player is *trying* to say to everybody, "I never miss that. This is so unusual that I missed that shot." Not very convincing. If she's in the outfield when the team is up by one run in the bottom of the ninth, the confident player says to herself, "Please let them hit me the ball. Let them hit it to me so I can catch it and make the final out"; whereas the unsure athlete says to herself, "Please don't let them hit it to me. Please don't let them hit it to me because I'll probably just mess it up and lose the game." Confidence is the key.

Buying into Acting <u>As If</u>

Tiffeny Milbrett loves the game of soccer and plays for the pure joy of it. She has never lacked confidence, but where she did need improvement was on her leadership ability and in her fitness level. She did not like to hear this, however. When I took her out of games at the seventy- or seventy-five-minute mark, she would ask, "Why am I coming out?" I would say, "Because you're only seventy minutes fit. When you get to be ninety minutes fit, I want you in there. But right now this fresh player is more dangerous to the opponent than you are." In time, through maturity and hearing it from enough people, Tiff worked to get to the level where she was a ninety-minute threat. She wasn't our fittest player, but she could score goals, as she did in the 2000 Olympic Gold Medal game in Sydney, at the ninetieth minute, to tie that game.

Tiffeny eventually bought into the way she had to be, and she acted *as if* she could survive the game and also dominate it in the eighty-ninth minute and score the key goals. She acted *as if* she were one of the fittest players and could carry her team late into the game. Brandi Chastain was the same way. Brandi believed she could run with them and so she did. She bought into the concept of fitness at the age of thirty or thirty-one and became one of our fittest players in 1999. She acted *as if* she could run with Kristine Lilly, Mia Hamm, Tisha Venturini and Carla Overbeck, all of whom were incredibly fit and displayed it constantly.

If you're coaching young girls, the goals don't really change, although they are on a lower plane. Young girls must be taught to buy into learning their role on the team, developing leadership skills and living up to their potential.

Instilling Confidence in Your Team

Confidence is an important issue with all players. To help instill confidence in them, you need to pick and choose your coaching moments. Quite obviously, you also need to make sure that the positive coaching greatly outweighs the negative coaching. You also have to be honest. Players can see through empty compliments and instead of instilling confidence, you'll probably end up reinforcing doubt.

Most people have trouble believing it, but Mia Hamm struggled with confidence. If you approached Mia and said, "Good game," it would be very upsetting to her if she felt that she hadn't played a *great* game. Instead, it was always better for you to say,

"Mia, you did a great job holding the ball in the attacking third of the field today." If, in fact, that was true, she *knew* it. But if you told her she had a great attacking game overall when she objectively didn't, instead of positively reinforcing confidence, the effect would be the opposite to her perception (and that of most players): *I didn't score any goals. What does he mean great attacking? I didn't get an assist, what's he talking about?* Instead, the trick was to pick out one thing she had done well in the attacking part of the field—something that was vital to the team, something she knew she had done well—and then praise it.

One of the techniques a coach can use to foster a team's confidence can be used at the end of each practice. Ask the team to arrange itself in a circle while stretching and cooling down. As the players are doing abdominal exercises, push-ups and other exercises, they are pretty much stationary targets. Walk over to each player and express whatever is on your mind. With our team, I might say something like, "Kate (speaking to Kate Sobrero), you ended up with a good group of players today, but your organization made that team so much better." And then I might walk over to Sara Whalen and say, "I've never seen you look faster going down the flank. They had absolutely no answer for you every time you got the ball." What you are trying to do is to reinforce an image of what these players did when they were successful. They probably realized they'd played well in those areas, but they need the coach to reinforce it, to let them know that you value their performance. But if you think it's a one-day process, you're mistaken. Some players never seem to lose confidence. But for most players it's a continual battle, an everyday effort.

A physical mistake is more apt to result in a loss of confidence than a mental mistake. Of course some coaches are quick to yank a player out of the game after she makes an error. Generally speaking, I don't think this is a good idea because it re-creates the negative spiral I've talked about earlier. The only time I'd ever take a player out for making a mistake would be for a mental lapse, if I thought she wasn't concentrating, for instance. But if a player mishits or miskicks a ball, well, my view is that we're all human. Soccer—and all sports, for that matter—is built on mistakes and failures and being able to overcome them. If you take someone out for a physical error, then you're negatively applying the dynamics of performance. Even how you respond to a mistake from the sidelines affects performance. For example, I could say to a player, "Shelly, Shelly, you've got to close that player quicker!" That's fine. But, if I say it sarcastically: "Oh, nice play, Shelly. That player just went around you again," then all I'm doing is diminishing Shelly's ability to play at peak performance.

You can't win by sarcastically criticizing one of your players. And you can't win if your players respond to their teammates with put-downs and negative comments. That behavior will only lower confidence levels instead of boosting them. If we, as coaches, see this kind of behavior, we have to expose it and address it. Don't get me wrong: It's acceptable for teammates to push each other and expect more of each other, but putting each other down hurts team performance.

Raising Team Confidence

In addition to dealing with the confidence of individual players, there are also times a coach has to address the team's confidence. A team as well as individual players has to act *as if*. You see this in professional sports all the time. Certain teams have auras of invincibility about them. Look at the New York Yankees. They have a mystique about them. Sure, they have great talent, but they also know how to win, so they do it consistently. They believe they can win and, as a result, they do. Our Women's National Team had that same aura. They acted *as if* they were the best team in the world, which, in the end, helped confirm that they *were* the best team in the world.

As a coach, there are times when you can help with team confidence. You might talk to the team and say things like, "I want to see you play today with an arrogance that lets the other team know that no one player can take you off the ball." Or you might say, "You're faster, you're stronger, you're better than the team you're facing today. Just go out and play your game."

Creating a successful team is all about teaching, shaping and fine tuning. It's about creating an environment where players truly *believe* they can perform at outstanding levels. Confident players focus on what they *can* do and don't worry about what they can't. Building confidence is about creating an environment in which a team truly *believes* it is a winner. It's about creating a safe environment where players can play on their cutting edge without fear of failure. As coaches, it's our job to help create that environment, to show the team that if they *act as if,* they can actually *be as if.* As the Buddhist saying encourages us: You must be the change you wish to see in the world.

COLLEEN'S TEAM-BUILDING EXERCISES

Triangle Tag

Objective

To require participants to protect and take responsibility for their teammates, cooperate with group members, use strategic deception to gain competitive advantage and project a confident appearance throughout the contest.

Equipment

None

Space

Several 10-yard grids (as in a football field) in which to maneuver

Number of Players

Groups of four

The Game

Three of the four players form a circle or a triangle. They link arms at the wrist, shoulders or elbows, and they are never allowed to break that connection. The fourth participant is outside the circle or triangle and is designated the tagger. One of the three in the triangle is designated the target and the job of the other two members of the triangle is to shuffle, move, spin and otherwise protect the target from being tagged. This competition continues for 15 seconds and then someone else is designated the tagger and the game continues. The goal is to have everyone take three turns being a protector and one turn being a tagger. Keep track of wins and losses as a protector and as a tagger so that all four players are competing for the best win-loss record.

Lesson

This is a game of intense physical competition. Players have to act as if they're doing one thing and then do another, fake one way and then go another. They have to act as if they are going to sneak over the back when they're really coming up from the bottom.

Debriefing

How competitive were you in this game? How competitive was your team?

How did you react when a teammate was tagged? How did that teammate react?

What does this exercise teach about winning and losing?

How did the tagger act when she was successful? When she was unsuccessful?

How do these lessons apply to the *Act as if* principle?

TONY'S CHALK TALK

Heading for Goals

Once the basic techniques of heading are established, then players can begin to learn how to pass, clear balls out of danger and score goals with their heads. Remember, it's part of a coach's job to eliminate the intimidation factor of heading so that your players become comfortable with attacking the ball and scoring head goals.

Exercise
Create grids of 8 yards by 12 yards (6 by 10 works great for younger players). There are two players on each team and they try to serve and head the ball through the goal with one of the opponents serving as a goalkeeper. The goalkeeper must stay on the goal line (don't allow them to come out away from the goal line and intercept the served or headed balls). The two attacking players must head the ball back and forth and then score by heading it past the goalkeeper and over the goal line. If it's headed above head height, it does not count. You want to teach players that when they head for goal, they want to head down. By making this simple rule that all goals must be head height or lower, you will be reinforcing heading the top center of the ball and heading down, where, in most cases, it's more difficult for the goalkeeper to save.

If a ball hits the ground, the other team takes over from where it fell and the first attacker hand serves a ball to the second attacker, who can head it directly into goal or head pass it back for the first attacker to shoot or pass.

Play this game for 3 minutes and then have winners match up against each other. The entire exercise should take less than 15 minutes, but the enjoyment level is high and the exercise encompasses a lot of technical training for heading.

Questions and Comments

Do players need to stand side by side and head the ball back and forth to work it down the field?

No, a player can move close to goal and the server can throw it so that it can be headed directly into goal. If the header chooses, she can head it back toward the server, but if she does the server must use only her head to score or pass.

What are the key coaching points of this exercise?

The player must watch the ball hit her forehead, then try to head the top center of the ball so that it goes down where the goalkeeper will have trouble saving it. Also, players must keep their mouths closed, hands out for balance and most important, use their legs, trunk and neck to head the ball with authority.

Coaching Challenge

Keeping it short and informative.

CHAPTER 13

Keeping the Main Thing the Main Thing

*Have a vision and then create your own reality. Otherwise, some-
one else may create it for you.*

— Tony DiCicco

The season is winding down, yet in a sense the hardest (and best)
part is yet to come: the playoffs or the big tournament. This is a
time when you and your team have an all-or-nothing mentality.
Every game counts. In effect, there is no tomorrow. You either win
now or it's that old Brooklyn Dodger chant, Wait till next year.

In order to win the big games that are on the horizon, you have
to know what's essential and what's peripheral. If the main thing is
peak performance, then you need to make sure both you and your
players say no to anything that might get in the way of that peak
performance. You cannot be distracted from your focus. This is
something I learned in 1995 when the team was in Sweden for my
first big international tournament as a head coach. The problem
became how distracting families could be to the team, which ultimately affected our on-field performance.

We always knew how supportive and uplifting family support-
ers were; we just didn't realize their potential downside. Husbands,
boyfriends, parents and friends were all staying at our hotel, and
they had traveled all that way to Sweden. Naturally they wanted to
see their wives, girlfriends, children and friends whenever possible.
Yet, during the World Cup competition, the days were already

pretty full for the players. We trained in the morning, we'd have our meals, we'd train again in the afternoon, then we'd have team meetings at night. After all those performance-related activities, it was time to go to bed and start the whole process over again the next morning. When would they possibly have time to socialize with their families?

What we learned from that situation was that we needed to instill in the team, a basic principle: Keep the main thing the main thing. We had to maintain focus on what we wanted to achieve and to this end we, the coaching staff, had to help the players remove any and all possible distractions.

So the following year, for the Olympics, Colleen initiated the Parents and Family Program. Colleen and my top assistant coach, Lauren Gregg, met with the parents after they arrived for our first Olympic game. First we told them how important it was for them to be there for support. We then explained that in our experience parents and friends often had questions such as, "Where do I pick up my tickets?" Or "Where can we park?" Or "When will we see you? How do we get to the venue? What time is your bus leaving?" These were all valid questions, but they were distractions for the players, taking the athletes away from what they should be focusing on: playing the best they could and winning.

Colleen prepared written guidelines that we wanted the players to follow during the Olympic Games as well as suggestions for friends and family members on how they could play a vital role in facilitating peak performances by our Olympic team. The plan we offered was to create a buffer at the team level. We chose Brandi Chastain's and Carla Overbeck's mothers to be liaisons, or ombudsmen, if you will. If a parent had a question, they now knew they could go to Lark or to Sandy and they'd get an answer. And if Sandy or Lark didn't have the answer, she could go to my team administrator or to Colleen to get the answer she needed.

In effect, we had created an environment where the coaches could coach and the players could play—in other words, our message was, "Let's keep the main thing the main thing." We created a filter between the parents and the players so that they never had to deal with those distractions. And the families got it: "We're not going to come to Tony and ask him where we can park. We're not going to go to our daughter and ask her what time the game is. We will find those answers elsewhere." As a result, in many ways, the parents felt more a part of the effort and more valuable as contributors to the team's success. Now they had a set of rules that governed their behavior and they knew they needed to abide by those rules for the good of the team. By following the established protocol, they were helping our collective effort and they were, of course, an important part of the team.

What really added to the equation was our sponsor Nike. They approached me during the buildup to the Olympics and asked how they could help. We spoke about their plans and then turned their hospitality location into a team location. Players and families would meet at a sorority house on the campus of the University of Georgia, where the semifinals and Gold Medal games were played. Nike brought in arcade games and catered food and installed a music system and a big-screen TV for watching the Olympic events. It was awesome, and it alleviated much of the anxiety of where and when to meet after games. There was no timetable; the parents visited the Nike Hospitality House to mingle with the other parents, and the players joined them at their leisure.

Of course, this procedure was implemented at a world-class level, but playoffs and a championship on an amateur level may be the Olympics for your age group. And if you have a vision of what you want to achieve, you as the coach have to make decisions that will help your team achieve it. Appropriate focus is what's important. Whether they are decisions about nutrition, training or lifestyle (things like staying out late at night or partying with friends), these are all examples of issues that have to be dealt with. The coach must create the optimal training rhythm for this team. During the period of time in which your team is training for the playoffs and championship, your players may have to make certain personal sacrifices. Even though most of the season might be over, they have to concentrate on training and on getting the job done. And the last thing they need are unnecessary and avoidable distractions.

How to Keep the Main Thing the Main Thing

Keeping the main thing the main thing means knowing what you want your team to achieve and helping your players know how they can best achieve it. It's all about commitment and goal setting. It's important that your players write down their goals because that forces them to make a promise to themselves. There have been studies that have found that fewer than 15 percent of business leaders write their goals down on paper. But that 15 percent represents 85 percent of the most successful business leaders.

As you head into the playoff and championship part of your season, take fifteen or twenty minutes during a practice and ask the team to write down the answers to the following questions. If your team is quite young, you may want to talk through the players' goals before they commit their answers to paper:

- What is your goal? At this point in the season the goal would be to win the championship.
- What is my plan to achieve this goal? Here you want the athletes to outline the step-by-step process, including actions they will take both as a team and as individuals. (You should also consider what steps you as coach need to make to help your team to succeed.)
- What observable and measurable actions must I add to my routine? For example, practice twenty minutes extra each day, get eight hours sleep a night, eat a healthy diet every day, and so on.
- How will I know if I'm doing a good job? Ask your players to keep track of their success in reaching their goals. Help them make any adjustments needed to help ensure that they are following a regimen that is appropriate to their skills, age and ability.

The Role of Parents in Keeping the Main Thing the Main Thing

The playoffs are an exciting time for players and for this reason it's easy for them to lose focus. Instead of focusing on the game itself, they are often distracted by socializing with friends or dealing with well-meaning parents who try to take their minds off the game by diverting them with a plethora of other activities. The best thing parents can do is help their child to focus on the task in front of them. Talk to them about the game. Ask them how they feel about it. Ask them how they think they can best help the team.

Another thing parents can do is to try to make their child's schedule a little less complicated. Today, we tend to overschedule our children, sending them from one extracurricular activity to another. This is fine, except that during the playoffs and championship game, it's best if the players are able to concentrate on soccer.

Remember, though, you're walking a thin line here, because the last thing you want to do is exaggerate the importance of the game by dwelling on it. Make your conversations casual and if you sense that your child is getting uptight, back off. And don't stop her from doing activities that have nothing to do with soccer. For parents the main goal is to create a well-rounded, happy child, not necessarily to put her on a career track, like becoming an Olympic gymnast or figure skater, where she has to spend most of her life at practice. I'm not saying that it isn't the right choice for some people, but there have been countless stories about how these decisions didn't end well for many families.

My son Alex is a great athlete, but he's also a very accomplished drummer. He loves music and he is honestly expecting Dave Matthews to call him up one day to take over for Carter Beauford at the drums. My wife and I are incredibly proud of him and how well-rounded he is. Any parent who has a family member playing drums knows that you have to be tolerant and carve out some time when (and where) they can practice. It's noisy and sometimes annoying, but as parents we need to assist our children and share in their goals and dreams. We can do that by helping them identify what their passions and interests are. Then we have to provide them with the tools to help them be disciplined and focused. I could have told Alex that he could never practice at home, or I could have severely limited when and where he played. But that wouldn't have helped him reach his goal and it wouldn't have taught him the importance of commitment and discipline.

These goals and dreams, of course, have to be our children's and not our own. There is a significant difference between the two and sometimes adults apply too much pressure to their children. They see things in terms of adult goals rather than goals appropriate to a child. A college professor once told me, "your first 35 years in life are experiments; then you can be serious about what you want to do." We can't expect our ten- and twelve-year-olds to get totally serious about what they want to do. They want to experiment, and they should. On one day your daughter will wake up and want to be a ballerina; on the next day she'll wake up and want to be a soccer star. Or you child will love playing soccer in the spring and then adore Little League Baseball in the summer. But that's okay. Kids often have one activity that's a priority and if both teams are practicing, then it's our job as parents to make sure they get to the practice for the number-one priority of the moment.

Another fact for parents to remember is that the main thing changes for most children because of the athlete's personal development as well as the influences of her age or peer group. Parents and coaches have to be aware of these factors and understand their impact. On the other hand, once a girl commits to playing soccer and her team is in the championship round, then she has to understand that she must stay focused and committed to the team, perhaps giving up other activities. She owes it to herself and to her teammates, at least for that season, to keep the main thing the main thing.

COLLEEN'S TEAM-BUILDING EXERCISES

All Aboard

Objective
To keep the main thing the main thing and not get sidetracked.

Equipment
Handkerchief, or a face towel folded to the size of a handkerchief

Space
Flat piece of ground

Number of Players
Ten to twelve on a team

The Game
Players are told that the main thing is to put one foot on the hand-kerchief/face towel while the other one is on the grass. If there isn't room, a player may put her foot on another girl's foot that's already on the handkerchief. Either way, the players may hold on to each other to accomplish this task. Once everyone has their feet on the handkerchief, they are told to pick the other foot up off the ground. They must remain completely on the handkerchief, balanced on one foot for three full seconds, holding on to their teammates during the process. The key is that one balanced foot cannot be touching the ground around the handkerchief and the other foot, the free foot, must be suspended in the air. They must keep trying this task until they succeed.

Lesson
Players will learn that they must focus on the task at hand and not let anything distract them. They must also communicate with each other to accomplish the goal.

Debriefing

What do you think this exercise accomplishes?

Which players assumed leadership roles in guiding your team? Were they successful?

What strategies did your team use to stay focused on the final goal?

Were you able to maintain your focus and concentration on the challenge at hand?

What did you learn from the experience?

How would you do it differently if you had the chance?

TONY'S CHALK TALK

Individual Defending

Coaching defense should be approached in three different ways: individual defending; group defending in the defensive, midfield and attacking thirds of the field; and team defending, in which all the players in all thirds of the field are moving together as the ball moves. In the following exercise you can set the foundation for overall defense by focusing on individual defending.

Exercise
Create two teams of four or five players (if you have more players create two different games). The field size is 30 yards by 20 yards with one big goal protected by a goalkeeper and one small goal without a goalkeeper.

A player from team A serves a ball from the 6-yard box to a player on team B who is standing by the small goal, which is outside the field dimensions. Encourage players to serve the ball in the air, not on the ground. When the team B player receives the ball, she attacks the big goal while the team A player defends. They play until the ball has been scored or is out of play. If the goalkeeper saves it, she distributes the ball to a team A player who tries to score on the small goal. As soon as one ball is dead, the next serve is made. The transition from offense to defense and back again is one of the keys of the game. Play for five minutes.

You can also play a variation of this exercise by having the attacking player start in front of the defender in a classic "back to goal" situation (a defender between an attacker and the goal). The attacker receives the ball from a teammate who is standing by the small goal out of play. The attacker must try to turn, go to the goal and score. The defender tries to prevent her from turning and facing the goal.

Questions and Comments

What are the keys for the defender?

In the first situation, the defender is moving up to confront an attacker who is coming at her. The defender must absorb the attacker by giving ground while waiting for an opportunity to tackle the ball. The key to the defensive technique is a staggered stance (one foot slightly in front of the other) and bending the knees, which lowers the center of gravity. The focus should be entirely on the ball. Defensive players should not be fooled by quick foot or body movements from the attacking player. Finally, make sure the defender is absorbing the forward movement of the attacker (giving ground) and assessing every touch by the attacker, looking for the time to pounce and tackle the ball.

In the second situation, the defender does not want to let the attacker turn. She must not get too close or the attacker will spin her out too far, thus allowing the attacker to turn and face the goal without challenge.

Coaching Challenge

Organization is the key. If you have lines of ten players, the game drags. Instead, put two games in play and bounce back and forth between them. After playing for 5 or 6 minutes have the teams change roles and keep score. If you have two games going on, have the two winners play each other. Make it competitive and it will be fun and a great learning exercise.

TONY'S CHALK TALK

Finishing Game

To develop players who are proficient scoring in front of the goal, coaches need to put their players in that part of the field so they will begin to feel comfortable. The following exercise, which is also excellent for goalkeeper training, is not only physically demanding, but it will also help develop your team's winning mentality.

Exercise
Play this game in the penalty area (the big rectangle in front of the goal). Create three teams with two players on each team. Two teams play while the other team helps retrieve balls. The game, which is a 2v2 with a goalkeeper, last only 3 minutes. Team A starts on defense and team B starts on offense. Team A tries to score. If the goalkeeper makes a save or team B steals the ball, they must pass it outside the penalty area to a coach or to one of the team C players. By passing the ball outside the area and getting it back, the two teams reverse roles. Team A becomes defensive and team B goes on the attack. The game is fast paced and coaches should encourage players to try to score with the fewest number of passes. You can also have two goalkeepers play. When team A is attacking, the team B goalkeeper defends and vice versa.

Questions and Comments

Can you play with more than two players on a team?
    Yes, 3v3 works but 4v4 may be too crowded. If there is no scoring taking place, reduce the numbers of players or add a plus player.

Coaching Challenges

The real challenge is to have as little down time as possible. If a ball is knocked out of bounds, another ball should immediately be played into the team that has earned possession. In other words, if team A takes a shot and it goes over the goal, team B should transition to offense immediately. To facilitate this, someone from outside the game must be ready to pass the ball in quickly.

Remember, encourage shooting and scoring with minimal passing.

CHAPTER 14

Is It Pressure or Is It Opportunity?

Don't get angry; get better.
—Tony DiCicco

Congratulations, you've made it to the championship round. After a long, hard season it's now down to only two teams and the big game is only a couple of days away. Anticipation is in the air and the excitement is building—but so is the pressure. Your players are being continually bombarded with questions like, "Is your team going to wilt under the pressure?" or "Do you think you can win it all?" At least that's how it was for us when we reached the Olympic finals. We were under the constant scrutiny of the media, fielding leading (and sometimes annoying) questions like, "You lost to Norway in 1995; now you're playing them in the semifinals of the Olympics. If you lose to them again, will this negate the fact that you beat them in the World Cup in 1991?"

Certainly the pressure was there. How could it not be? We were playing in the first-ever women's Olympic soccer final, in front of the largest crowds we'd ever faced, and playing against one of the best teams in the world. All of these factors were hard to ignore, especially while we mingled with sports legends like Monica Seles, Billie Jean King, Michael Johnson and the Dream Team at the opening ceremonies. In addition to those distractions, we also had to deal with our share of adversity. Mia went down in one game with an ankle injury and Brandi suffered a knee injury in another.

Were we adversely affected by the pressure? I don't think so. And with good reason.

In preparation for the 1996 Olympic Games we never talked about pressure because we saw the tournament as an opportunity to prove that we were the best women's soccer team in the world. We knew that as soon as we allowed the word "pressure" into the equation, the process would revolve around avoiding pitfalls and barriers to our goals and, inevitably, we would lose focus. Instead of playing with freedom and confidence, with imagination and exuberance, we would spend our time trying to avoid making mistakes—a sure recipe for disaster.

In the end, we dealt with the pressure well and won the tournament, playing like a true world championship team. But winning the Olympic Gold Medal was just the beginning. After 1996, the Women's National Team became far more visible and well-known not only in the United States but also throughout the world. As a result, the eyes of the nation and the international sport world were focused even more closely on us. I didn't think anything could be bigger than the Olympics, but the World Cup in 1999 actually overshadowed the Olympics. That competition became so monumental and attracted so much media, including TV exposure, that pressure was an undeniable part of it. Now the stakes were raised even higher and the media was at it again! "What if you don't get to the finals?" "Will we ever have a Women's Professional League?" Suddenly the weight of women's professional soccer was laid squarely on our shoulders.

The pressure was palpable and yet, in retrospect, I'm not sure we were even aware of it because we were having so much fun. We certainly didn't walk around tight-lipped with our fists perpetually clenched. There were periods, I'm sure, when everyone on the team must have felt pressure, although those moments were surrounded by periods of total elation. After all, given the choice, where else in the world would we have wanted to be?

But we didn't get to that point without work. We spent a great deal of time talking about our opportunities and how they overshadowed the pressure. And we trained the team in handling the press. When somebody from the media would ask, "Is the pressure getting to be overwhelming?" the players would answer, "We don't think of it as pressure. We think of it as opportunity."

Positive Substitution

In order to deal with the negative consequences of pressure, you have to teach your players to substitute some other positive vision for it. Instead of focusing on the enormity of the task ahead, try to *feel* the rewards of what you're going to reap. Once again Colleen and I used the same imagery techniques we had used to encourage the players to keep their eyes on the prize. These were the kinds of opportunities we used to replace all the potential negative pressures associated with the World Cup, including the prospect of early elimination or of having the entire event be viewed as unsuccessful because the U.S. team wasn't in the finals. It wasn't easy, but we were able to do it.

Obviously we were competing at a much higher level and with much more at stake than most teams, but it's important to understand that pressure doesn't distinguish playing in the World Series or the World Cup from the pressure of playing in a tournament final at the under-twelve level or a high school championship game. It's still *pressure*. For that fifteen-year-old girl playing in the state championship game, the pressure she feels is every bit as intense and as potentially limiting as the pressure Kristine Lilly or Brandi Chastain felt.

As coaches, staff and parents we can add pressure or we can help peel it away. It all depends on how you address the situation. Here are some techniques that Colleen taught us to help us relax and deal with pressure:

- Smile. The signal that smiling sends to your body and your subconscious is that things are fine. When you frown or clench your fists, the message is that there's a problem. As coach, no matter how tense the situation may be, you ought to make sure that you smile when you're around your team. This will not only relax them, but it will also communicate confidence. Smiling is contagious and if they see you smile chances are they will too, which will send the appropriate message to their subconscious.

- Sigh. Sighing acts to release tension. I used this one myself many times and I remember walking down the hall one day and bumping into Kristine Lilly at the elevator. I gave a big sigh and Lil smiled and said, "Oh, Tony, I see you're using one of those pressure-relieving techniques that Colleen taught us."

- Keep reminding your team that it's fantastic that they've gotten as far as they have and now is the time to relax, have fun and enjoy every minute of the experience. And make sure your staff is doing the same thing.

- Keep things in perspective. I guarantee that every one of the 1999 Women's National Team players felt less pressure in the finals than they did in the semifinals or quarterfinals. Earlier rounds in a major tournament are distinct in that if you lose in the quarterfinals, you have no way to redeem yourself. You literally leave the tournament the next day. It's much more pressure to get to the finals than it is to actually play in the ultimate game you've won the right to play in.

- Find helpful distractions to take your players' minds off worrying about the game. When we were making the Olympic run, the players kidded me by suggesting that if they won, I'd have to shave off my moustache. Between the semifinal and the Gold Medal game, the deal came up again, but I didn't really pay much attention to it. The day after our victory, the players were prepared to drag me into the bathroom to shave it off. Finally I relented and off it went, the first time I'd been without it since my senior year in college, 1969–1970. The funniest part of this came some days later when I was on a television talk show and my wife and son Nicholas, who was five at the time, were home watching. When I came on the screen and my wife said, "Nicholas, there's Daddy," he started crying and said, "That is not my daddy."

- Display confidence. As a leader, it's your job to set a confident tone while at the same time showing exhilaration and joy.

- Be specific about what has to be done in the game. "We'll beat this team, and win this championship, if we do this, this and this—all things we're capable of doing. We've done these things all season long. This is a good team we're up against and we need to respect them, but if we do this, this and this, we'll be champions."

- Talk about the pressure. It's a good idea to have a team meeting in which players can share their feelings about how the pressure feels. And during that session allow all your players to express themselves, especially those with a good sense of humor. On our team, Julie Foudy, as serious a competitor as she is, was always kidding around, laughing and cracking jokes—a great way to resolve pressure. As I've said before, if you're laughing, it's hard to feel pressure.
- If it ain't broke, don't fix it. Don't change the training method that got you to the championship game in the first place. The only change I might make would be to add a specific team meeting to help with the mental preparation for the game.

One fact we, as parents and coaches, must remember is that kids pick up cues from us. If we walk around with stern looks on our faces, if we seem tense and uptight, if we seem to be taking winning and losing as a matter of life and death, then naturally our players will adopt this attitude. We need to inventory just what it is we want from the sport experience and why we want it. Do we want our children to win for them, or for us? The answer is, of course, that we should want them to win because it will make them feel good, but part of making them feel good is relieving as much pressure as we possibly can. That's what will make the whole experience fun, memorable and exciting. Win or lose, the experience a team gains from training together, working hard to reach a collective goal and giving everything they have to accomplish their dreams, is one they will carry for a lifetime.

COLLEEN'S TEAM-BUILDING EXERCISES

Wolves and Sheep

Objective

To reveal those players willing to take a risk and those who aren't. This is an exercise you can use to get fit without making it a boring and painful experience. It's also an opportunity to see how your players respond under pressure. What you hope for is that players will embrace both levels of opportunity: to get fit and to outfox their opponents.

Equipment

Cones or lines to designate a playing area. You will also need cones to designate the safety box.

Space

The dimensions should allow for 5 yards per participant. For example, for a four-on-four game (eight players), the field should be at least 40 yards long. You can vary the length and width to accommodate the size, age and aerobic capacity of the competitors.

Number of Players

Any number

The Game

Divide your group into two equal teams. Give each team a name, for example, Reds and Blues. At any two diagonal corners of the rectangular field, create two safety zones. These zones should be squares that use two of the playing field sidelines, with cones being placed to complete the square inside the playing area (consider a 5-by-5 yard space as a starting point). Players from both teams jog, run, sprint or skip (your choice) around the inside of the playing area. After unpredictable intervals of time, for example, 1 minute, 30 seconds, 90 seconds, 10 seconds yell out one team's name.

At that point all the Reds become "wolves" and try to chase all the members of the other team, who are now the "sheep," and tag as many as they can before the sheep can get safely inside the safety zones. The important point to remember is that the team you call will be the ones who will do the chasing. Once a player is tagged, he joins the other team. Players are safe if they can run to a safety zone without being tagged.

Make sure you vary the order of the teams called to be the wolves in some unpredictable way. How quickly and how often you call a team name should be as random and variable as possible.

When all of one team has been captured by another team, the game ends.

Variation

You can have players dribble a basketball, soccer ball, or run with a football while they are chasing and being chased. Use your imagination!

Debriefing

What did you learn about the relationship between risk taking and playing it safe and secure?

How did it feel when you were chasing your opponent? Being chased? What do you think that difference means?

How did skill and tactics factor into success, rather than sheer speed and quickness?

What would you do differently next time?

How does this exercise pertain to the championship game?

CHAPTER 15

The Power of One

I have not only seen the heart of the champion on Olympic and World Cup fields; I've also seen it every time I've witnessed a Youth Soccer game.

— TONY DiCicco

Although soccer is a team sport, it's still made up of individuals. Individuals have to work together to create a winner, but it's also important to remember that one person can—and often does—make a difference. What we're talking about here is the power of one. This is especially important in terms of a championship game. Obviously, the team has to play together as a team, but it's also an opportunity for one, two, three or even more of your players to step up and take charge.

Two of the questions Colleen insisted our players ask themselves were:

- What is your influence on the team?
- What is your influence on the game?

Her point was simple: Each person exerts a powerful influence on the environment and on others, so instead of focusing on your rights and your entitlements, focus on your responsibilities. Take control. Take responsibility. "Like a pebble into a smooth lake," she said, "the ripple effect of your actions carry on to infinity. No thoughts, no words, no actions are neutral; they all have an effect. The only question is, What will the effect be?"

When you talk to your team about *the power of one*, you are trying to convey two meanings. One is that each player should take responsibility for herself. The other is that the team's efforts should be calculated, coordinated and well choreographed. In other words, at some point in the season, and it should have happened by the time the playoffs have rolled around, the group of individual players has become a finely tuned team unit whose whole is greater than the sum total of all the parts.

The individual still plays an important part in this equation, however. The question each player has to ask herself is, "How can I, as just one player, make this team better?" This is the challenge all coaches face: motivating players to constantly improve themselves, to take more *responsibility* and not worry about what their rights and entitlements are. They should focus on what they can contribute, how they can serve their teammates or the organization and how they can bring out the best in themselves and others.

Gro Espeseth from Norway is a perfect example. I knew Gro very well because I coached against her for a decade. A fierce competitor, she came back from Sydney where she won an Olympic Gold Medal in 2000, and helped launch the Women's United Soccer Association in 2001. Playing for the New York Power alongside Tiffeny Milbrett, she found herself in the semifinals against Brandi Chastain and the CyberRays. During the first half there was a collision in front of the Power goal, and Gro suffered a severe gash to her forehead. From the broadcast booth near the top of the stadium you could see the blood clearly flowing down her face. She was escorted off the field and I expected her to be finished for the day. As it turned out, she would require twenty stitches to close the cut, but she wasn't going to get them until after the game. Instead, Gro came back into the game before the end of the half. Obviously injured, she was still running up field on set pieces as the target person to serve balls to so that she could win them with her head and play them into the goal mouth. Her team was clearly inspired and they tied the game just before halftime. Gro started the second half as well, but eventually she did have to come out of the game and the

CyberRays went on to defeat the New York Power 3–2. But not before Gro had made her statement.

After the game I made it a point to speak with her. "What were you thinking?" I asked.

"I could not let my team down; I must be there for them and give all of myself."

I simply smiled. I had always had a great deal of respect for Gro, but never more than I had at that moment.

What we as coaches and parents ought to teach our players, not only on the field but also in anything they do, is to stand out, to take risks and do things that might be on the cutting edge. We want them to shun mediocrity and seek excellence. Obviously, when an athlete takes risks, there is always the chance of failure, but a can-do attitude often results in taking talent to a higher level.

TRY

One of the many wonderful concepts Colleen introduced to the team was an acronym she called TRY—take responsibility yourself. The idea was simple and yet it was essential to our becoming a successful winning team.

Every person, whether in sports or not, who wants to be successful has to identify and then develop ways in which her impact can be greatest. This feat can be accomplished through a combination of discipline, a strong work ethic and by studying the subject carefully. In the end, there are myriad ways that individuals can take personal responsibility for those factors directly under their own control. For example, I may not be able to control whether I score a goal or not, but I can control whether I execute a skill properly, whether I'm as fit as I can be and whether I play within the team concept. Players can and should take individual responsibility for these aspects of their game. It is important that each athlete commit to improving her own level of performance and contribution and only then will the *power of one* have an impact on the entire team.

If you can encourage your players to give their ultimate effort not only in big games, like the championship, but also every day in practice, while at the same time maintaining a strong ethic of working together for the good of the team, then the chances of success are tremendously enhanced. For example, in many games Briana Scurry barely had to make a save. Yet she was always ready and well trained for that key game in which she might make the difference. And that time came in the semifinals against Brazil during the 1999 World Cup. We won that game 2–0, but anyone present knew the margin of victory was the goalkeeping. Briana was nothing short of inspiring. And then, in the final, Briana once again came up with the key save during the penalty kick shoot-out that again was the margin of victory. By stepping up when she had to, Briana showed the *power of one* while she took on responsibility for the team at the same time. The result was that along with Michelle Akers, Briana was our MVP during those last two games.

As a coach, it's your responsibility not only to teach teamwork but also to make it clear to your players that part of their responsibility to the team is to use their own *power of one* to help the rest of their teammates reach the ultimate goal, in this case emerging victorious in the championship game.

COLLEEN'S TEAM-BUILDING EXERCISES

Human Dragon

Objective
To take the responsibility to work hard to stay connected, to anticipate the next move and to protect the tail of the dragon. On the surface this looks like a team game and in some ways it is. Yet each individual player affects the outcome of the exercise.

Equipment
None needed

Space
An open field or gym, free from obstacles

Number of Players
Divide your group into four teams of six to eight individuals. You can have odd numbers and you can vary the length of the "dragon," depending on the skill, size and ability of your athletes.

The Game
Each team designates the "head" person and the "tail" section of the human dragon. Team members fill in behind the head of the dragon by holding on to the person in front of them at the waist. At this point, your four dragon teams should form four separate long lines with the members of each dragon connected by holding on to each other's waists in a single-file line.

The goal of the activity is for the head of each dragon to attempt to tag the tail of any other dragon team. Only heads of the dragon can do the tagging, since all other team members must remain connected (with two hands) to their teammates. Players attempt to avoid having their team's tail tagged, and skillfully (did I mention, humorously?) try to shield their tail from other dragons on the prowl.

Each time a tag occurs, the tagging team receives one point and the tail of the team that was tagged becomes the new dragon head, creating a new tail. If one person is a tail for too long, switch the tail at periodic time intervals. If any of the dragon people in the middle release their grip on the person in front of them, teams are asked to self-report the loss of a point for their team. At that moment, teams should again switch the tail of the dragon. Dragons should call out their score every time they gain or lose a point. The game continues as competitiveness and interest allows.

Lessons
This team-building exercise helps to develop communication, competition, honesty, cooperation and protection of teammates. By moving as a team to protect their tail, the team's success is more likely enhanced. It is a simple, entertaining initiative in which the following concepts can be emphasized and developed:

• Collective effort
• Competition between groups
• Cooperation within groups
• Individual responsibility

This challenge is an excellent small-group activity whose difficulty can be altered to achieve desired results. For example, groups can be prodded to beat the other teams or to beat their own group's personal record, depending on (a) an extrinsically oriented focus on outcome and result or (b) the desire to emphasize intrinsically motivated standards of excellence. Decide what's best for your group at this particular point in your training cycle and alter the activity to meet those demands.

Debriefing
What is the relationship between the head of the dragon and the body of a dragon? How about between the head and the tail? What about all three components together?
What happens when different parts of the dragon have different plans of action for how to be successful?

How did you react to the challenge of tagging the other dragons?

How did you respond when you were tagged either as a team or as an individual?

What does it take to play this game successfully?

What does it illustrate about the power of one?

How does individual performance impact team success?

How can we apply these lessons to our season?

TONY'S CHALK TALK

Create Scoring Chances by Changing the Point of Attack

As players get older and defenses get more organized, attacking play must become more sophisticated. It's not good enough to simply force the ball through the heart of the defense to your best athlete. You have to coach your team on how to probe and look for the openings and, once they find one, to strike quickly before the defense can regroup. Your team can do this by changing the point of the attack—for instance, by trying the right side if the middle is clogged, then switching to the left side before the defense can shift effectively. The idea is to teach your players to improvise and the following exercises will help them to do just that.

Change of Point Game

The field should be approximately 30 yards long by 65 yards wide. There is a goal, about 6 yards wide, placed 10 yards in from each corner so that each team can attack two goals, one at one end of the field and one at the other end of the field.

This game, which is also a great game for defensive work in the midfield, should be played with a 7v7 or 6v6+2 (the maximum numbers are probably 8v8+1). The +2 are always offensive players. Let them play for a few minutes and, slowly, try to get them to read the defense. Ask them, "If there are five of the seven defenders close to this goal, then what do you think we should do?" After a while, they will start to understand how to play to the open goal. If the game is organized properly, you will start to see a different mind-set as to how to break down the defense. They will see that once the defense thinks your team will play across the field, then vertical passing lanes may very well open up.

Questions and Comments

How long should I play this game?

This game is demanding especially if you have a smaller number of players, so I wouldn't play it beyond 15 minutes, maybe even less the first couple of times.

What are the key coaching points?

Vision is a key asset to any soccer player. Your players should be asking themselves questions such as "If I'm receiving a ball from close to this goal, can I see the other side of the field, where my teammates are, where the opponents are and the exact location of the goal we want to attack?" If she can see those things, explain to her that she has increased her range of play and will be able to make better decisions for her team.

Should the players be able to pass the ball from one side of the field to the other?

Only the most technical players will have that ability, so there needs to be a combination of short and long passes and quick player movement to get to the new goal as quickly as possible.

Coaching Challenge

Whenever you are coaching tactics, the key is to create decision-making opportunities. Ask yourself if you are assisting your players in recognizing the options and making the right decisions. Remember, soccer is a tactical game, yet at the same time it's very active, demanding, competitive and a lot of fun.

CHAPTER 16

Players', Parents' and Coaches' Boot Camp: What to Do in the Off-season

I love my job!
—Tony DiCicco

The season is over. Whether you've won the championship or not, it's still been a successful run because you've seen your team grow, play hard, win and, most important, have fun. But the work isn't over yet. In many ways, it's just begun because off-season preparation is critically important in determining how your team will perform next season.

For Players

Cross-Training

As a coach you're going to have to answer questions from your players about what kinds of sports you think they should be involved with in the off-season. Your responses are important because some sports help hone skills that are particular to soccer while others will simply keep your athletes in better overall physical shape while providing an emotional alternative to the rigors of a competitive soccer season. But whatever sport the girls choose, cross-training is an important ingredient for the off-season. Not only will it help keep your players fresh athletically, but it will also give them a break from their primary discipline, which can help sustain and extend their motivation into the next season.

When I look at some of the incredible athletes I coached during my tenure as National Team coach, I see players like Christie Pearce, who was on a basketball scholarship at Monmouth College in New Jersey, and Tiffany Roberts, who was an awesome track star during her high school career in California. When Tiff was still in high school and we were training with the National Team in California, I saw her in the hall and instead of being her usual smiling self, I could sense something was on her mind. After speaking with me for a few moments, she finally opened up and asked, "Do you think Anson would mind if I missed practice tomorrow and went to the high school state track and field championship instead? It's being held not far from here." I said, "Let's go speak to Anson," knowing that Anson would be totally supportive because he knew that track and field was a discipline that had crossover skills for soccer and because he knew that Tiff, like many other players, needed a break from her primary sport. Even though we had trained very hard for the past two days, Tiffany went to her track meet to run the 800-meter event and finished second in the state.

• Periodization

It's very important that coaches make sure their players examine their entire schedule of competition for the year, which includes being concerned about what they do in their down time away from the competitive season. Most athletes follow a training technique called periodization. For an athlete, down time, meaning time when their primary season ends, doesn't mean sitting on the couch and watching TV. Instead, it might mean zeroing in on fitness-related activities (this would be gym workouts, for example) three times a week or cross-training exercises, like riding a bicycle, running or playing a sport like basketball, volleyball or lacrosse instead of soccer.

Soccer is one of those sports, like gymnastics, that requires maintaining a certain skill level all year long, even if you're not playing the game every day. As a goalkeeper, I didn't have to play soccer all year round. I could take part in a variety of other sports that would facilitate my goalkeeping and help keep me fresh and motivated for the next soccer season. For instance, I could play basketball or volleyball because the skills that are necessary for success in those sports can also be applied to soccer goalkeeping. But it was important that, being as serious about soccer as I was, the sports I chose to play did, in fact, relate to soccer in some way. If you are a dedicated soccer player, it's best to choose off-season sports that will add to your development of the skills or fitness vital to the game.

If you're going to become a good soccer athlete, even though you're engaged in other activities (which I encourage), you've got to make sure that your plan for soccer is a priority and well thought out. If it's too vague or if you're only playing soccer a few months out of the year and you don't have a specific plan in place, then you're going to be losing ground to all those kids who are playing soccer in a more focused or year-round schedule. Without a doubt, cross-training is incredibly important, but you have to look at the individual first to find out where her starting point is. For instance, if you have a girl who plays soccer in the fall and spring and basketball all winter, you probably don't need to worry about encouraging more cross-training for her because she's getting that effect from her other sport. On the other hand, for a girl who plays fall and spring soccer and then indoor soccer in the winter, you've got to find a place during her schedule for rest and alternative types of training. In that case you'd want to encourage some kind of cross-training regimen, perhaps some time in the gym working in the weight room, on the exercise machines or out on the track.

Which Sport Should They Play?

There's no one perfect answer as to which off-season sports young women should play. I think every individual is different, and my family is a perfect example of that principle. One of our sons is a great all-around athlete who could easily play high school basketball. But for him, the *only* thing he wants to do is play soccer. It's always been a battle for me to get him to consider other activities to enhance his still-growing musculature. I suggest everything from fast footwork exercises to weight training and more recreational sports like snowboarding—all of which provide diversity and cross-training opportunities. Regardless of what I suggest, though, he's able to find a soccer game no matter what time of the year it is.

I'm a strong believer in multisport experiences, especially for younger athletes under the age of fourteen. While I have trouble getting our one son to play other sports, my three other sons participate in several different sports, and they don't seem to favor any particular one. Obviously, there isn't one model that's right for every child.

Participating in different sports helps round off muscle development in young bodies, and it also gives the child a psychological break from the rigor of participating in only one sport. I'm not saying a child ought to play five different sports, although that's certainly okay, but if your child plays soccer year-round, eventually her desire for the game will burn out or she will run a higher risk of injury. Soccer may be her main and favorite sport, but elite athletes know that they will develop faster and further using cross-training techniques and activities to complement their number-one sport.

For girls primarily interested in soccer, I would suggest the following cross-training sports:

- If you want your player to enhance fitness, there's nothing better than track, especially sprint training for anaerobic fitness and running the longer distances for aerobic fitness.
- For understanding how to play individual defense, basketball and lacrosse are great. They also allow young players to develop power and quickness requirements that are similar to soccer. These sports actually have many of the same natural plays, like wall passes in soccer or the give and go in basketball and lacrosse.
- For girls between the ages of twelve and fourteen who see soccer as their primary sport, I'm a strong believer in basketball, field hockey, lacrosse or track. Volleyball is another good option because one of the key physical properties of that sport is that it helps develop power. Power or the execution of strength with a time component is also a critical aspect of soccer conditioning. In

other words, to be able to lift 100 pounds is one thing, but to be able to do it with speed in repetition is something even more applicable to the development of a soccer player. The example I use is when a basketball player goes up for a rebound and keeps the ball alive by tapping it off the board. The player comes back down but is then the first one back up there to secure the ball. That's a demonstration of power. And that power factors into your first step and your first 5-yard sprint in soccer. Both are incredibly important in developing an explosive first step on the soccer field. The development of power also factors into your ability to jump and to accelerate laterally, which are also incredibly important assets in soccer.

- You may also suggest some strength training for your players during the off-season, depending on the age of the athlete. We consistently followed an appropriately designed weight-training program with our athletes, even during the season, including the buildup time period prior to major competitions. Weight training is certainly useful in soccer because it helps to prevent injuries and build power, strength and flexibility. Some kids love to get into a weight room, but other kids, and I was one of them, need a ball and a team to be motivated to train. But you don't have to go into a weight room to do strength training. Instead, you can step out onto the field and work with any resistance exercise program. If your players do decide to work with weights, you must impress upon them the need to have a knowledgeable person develop an appropriate program for them. Age, the presence or absence of injury and even the point you're at in the competitive season are just a few of the variables that should be considered prior to beginning a program. Players shouldn't just go into the local fitness center and start working on the machines without supervision and qualified direction from a knowledgeable professional.

- To build stamina, the sports that instantly come to mind are indoor or outdoor track, field hockey, lacrosse, cross-country running, swimming and basketball. The reason I personally favor basketball is that from a tactical standpoint, many of the moves are quite similar to soccer. Playing 5v5 soccer is like playing basketball, except that the player's feet are on the ground instead of in the air. Swimming is a good activity because it tends to elongate muscles, which is very good for flexibility.

- For strength I suggest track, especially the sprint events—the 100-, 200-, 400- or even 800-meter races—which are excellent for anaerobic endurance and also help strengthen the legs. These disciplines usually involve doing six to ten sprints in a training session which, when compared to the amount of sprinting a player does in soccer, provides athletes with the ability to recover quickly and immediately go 100 percent again. That ability is really the ultimate definition of soccer fitness. If I sprint twenty times for 30 yards, my last sprint compared to my first sprint will give me an indication of my aerobic fitness level.

- When it comes to eye-foot coordination, you are not going to get much correlation from any sport to help your soccer skills. For hand-eye coordination, however, any sport that uses a ball is helpful.

Remember, alternatives with variety and diversity are important ingredients to sustaining interest and helping to ensure a well-rounded individual, both as an athlete and as a person.

For Parents

One of the best things you can do for a child is help her identify her long-range goals. Once she's chosen those goals, you can help her make a plan of how to get there. If your daughter wants to be a great soccer player, then you have to make sure she's playing enough quality soccer. This challenge may mean not only playing on her high school team but also competing on a club team, attending soccer camp in the summer, or even finding a qualified coach who can give her private lessons.

Tracy Ducar, a member of the World Cup championship team, had been a student of mine when she was in high school. I followed her career from high school to the University of North Carolina and eventually onto the U.S. National Team. I experienced some of the ups and downs during her journey, but Tracy always impressed me by the fact that she had a plan, knew how to carry it out and would not let anything deter her from her dreams. One of my most painful decisions as a coach was when I had to replace Tracy as the reserve goalkeeper for the Olympic team in 1996. She had suffered an injury shortly before my decision had to be made and I felt that I owed it to the team to have a reserve goalkeeper who was 100 percent. Tracy was devastated, angry and confused, but through her dedication and determination, she rebounded and made the 1999 World Cup team. One of the primary reasons she was able to do this was because she had an intricate plan to help her reach her goal of recovering from her injury and again playing soccer on an elite level. Today Tracy is the goalkeeper for the Boston Breakers in the WUSA.

Recently a parent, whose daughter plays soccer, told me that the family was going to England during February and asked if I had any contacts over there because they wanted to attend a soccer game. Interestingly enough, the parents aren't soccer players nor are they particularly ardent fans, but their daughter is. As parents, they're developing an appreciation for the game that they can now share with their daughter and are exposing her to a brand of soccer she might not be able to see here in the United States. At the same time they are sending her a very supportive message, in essence saying, We take your goals seriously and we want to help you attain them.

Soccer can and often does become a family activity. You're more likely to reach the highest level of performance if you all appreciate and cultivate a knowledge of this beautiful game. Certainly this supportive and active involvement is preferable to simply acting the part of taxi driver as you shuttle your child back and forth between practice and games.

For Coaches

Make no mistake about it, coaching is a significant responsibility. A good part of that responsibility requires spending some time developing the knowledge and skill of how to teach the sport. One of the most important activities a coach can engage in during the off-season is setting specific goals for the following season. When you set goals, what you're doing is identifying what you want to achieve and developing a plan as to how you're going to get there. It's like planning a car trip. Before you decide on the best route, you have to know what your destination is. There is an important difference between setting high or difficult goals and setting impossible goals. You have to have realistic aspirations but also be careful not to limit those aspirations. When you set these goals you are, as my wife likes to say, creating your own reality. In other words, you are explicitly identifying what you're looking for in life, instead of keeping those dreams hidden someplace in your subconscious.

In terms of whether you, as a coach, have had a successful season, you ought to revisit those goals you set at the beginning of the season to see how close you came to reaching them.

- Are you the kind of coach you wanted to be? Look back at the season and ask yourself if your playing style has helped your athletes succeed. Ask yourself if your coaching style has been successful in terms of getting the best out of all your players.
- Were you successful dealing with your players, helping them reach their potential? Look at every player. See which ones have improved and which haven't. Ask yourself if you have created leadership within your team. Analyze how you can improve your approach to dealing with your players.
- Ask yourself if the style of play you taught fits your team. Have you, for instance, coached your team for speed that your players don't have? If so, perhaps you ought to think about adjusting it to work with the abilities of the players on the team.
- Has your team reached its full potential? Examine the athleticism of the girls on your team to see if they're playing as well as they could.
- Compare the level of development of your team against the teams you play. Is your team consistently playing catch-up? Is your team beating the opposition too easily? Your course of action for next year should be based on your answers. If you lost

every game, perhaps you need to speak to the organizers of the league and ask to go down a level. If your team is winning all its games, perhaps you should ask to be placed in a more challenging league.

- Ask yourself, Where do I need to improve as a coach? Is it in the realm of tactics? Physical fitness training? Communicating with players?

From a coach's standpoint, obviously there's nothing more rewarding than working with a young team and seeing that team respond positively to your coaching as you help them perform at a higher level. Winning or losing is not the primary factor; the focus is on facilitating their growth as players and as people. For these outcomes to happen, coaches need to make an investment well beyond the parameters of the season. Here are some suggestions for contributing to your own knowledge of the game.

- One of the best ways to enhance skills, whether it be coaching or playing, is to put yourself into the proper environment as frequently as possible. I'm the kind of person who learns from watching, then doing; so to this day I still watch all the soccer I can. For instance, if I'm anywhere near a professional soccer club while traveling, I'll make it a priority to watch practice sessions. I can always learn something new. I also watch the international games on cable TV because so much of my coaching comes from observing the best players in the world who are absolute geniuses on the soccer field. They do things I'm sure no one has ever taught them. They seem to perform these tactics instinctually. I watch these players and say to myself, *That's awesome. I want to take that move or that tactic and teach it to my players.*
- Young coaches, and I'm even talking about parent coaches, can pick up helpful tips for training at workshops, symposia and soccer conventions. You may also learn any number of entertaining exercises that will help instill an appreciation and love for the game of soccer as well as also help players improve their skills.
- Playbooks or books on tactics and the like as well as videos and CD ROMs are all valuable teaching and learning tools. Again,

this is an easy, accessible way to immerse yourself in the sport environment and often leads to helping to generate fresh ideas of your own.

Both Colleen and I can honestly say that coaching has enriched our lives beyond anything either of us could have ever dreamed possible. It's helped us evolve as more complete, energized and appreciative human beings. Our greatest hope is that it does as much for you.